Gospel Light's

DISCOVERY LAB
CRAFTS FOR KIDS

Includes Projects for Children from Preschool to Sixth Grade:

✳ Colorful Projects with a Scientific Invention Theme

✳ Reproducible Awards and Certificates

✳ Bible Memory Verse Coloring Posters

Compiled By Kim Sullivan Fiano

How to Make Clean Copies from This Book

You may make copies of portions of this book with a clean conscience if

- you (or someone in your organization) are the original purchaser;
- you are using the copies you make for a noncommercial purpose (such as teaching or promoting your ministry) within your church or organization;
- you follow the instructions provided in this book.

However, it is ILLEGAL for you to make copies if

- you are using the material to promote, advertise or sell a product or service other than for ministry fund-raising;
- you are using the material in or on a product for sale; or
- you or your organization are not the original purchaser of this book.

By following these guidelines you help us keep our products affordable.

Thank you,

Gospel Light

Library of Congress Cataloging-in-Publication Data applied for.

Gospel Light

Publisher, William T. Greig
Senior Consulting Publisher, Dr. Elmer L. Towns
Publisher, Research, Planning and Development, Billie Baptiste
Managing Editor, Christy Weir
Associate Editors, Kim Sullivan Fiano, Karen Stimer
Assistant Editor, Linda Bossoletti
Contributing Writers, Linda Crisp, Kathryn Frey, Loreen Robertson, Dianne Rowell
Contributing Editors, Melanie Austin, Linda Crisp, Sheryl Haystead, Susan Ludes, Jan Worsham
Designer, Carolyn Thomas
Illustrator, Anne Stanley

Contents

Introduction to *Discovery Lab Crafts for Kids* 4
Crafts with a Message 4
Be Prepared 5
Craft Symbols 5
Lab Notes 5
GP4U Crafts 5
Helpful Hints 6

Introduction to "Discovery Lab Crafts for Kids"

Fun in the Inventor's Lab

God is the ultimate creator and He created people to be extraordinarily inventive as well. From the beginning of time, people have created the most incredible contraptions out of ordinary objects—small machines that record voices, large machines that transport people thousands of miles, glass lenses to help you see across the street or all the way to the moon. God designed an entire world and universe for us to discover. It's no wonder that children are born inventors! That's why your children will love to invent and experiment with the arts and crafts found in this resource book, *Discovery Lab Crafts for Kids.*

As your children create their own inventions and learn about science, they'll discover the world God created and the reason He created us. In the beginning God had a plan, and it includes each adult and child. As children create their crafts together, look for times to affirm that God loves them so much that He provided a way for us to be with Him forever. Talk about the ways God shows His love to us. Give them opportunities to ask questions.

We hope that you and your students will enjoy many fun-filled hours creating these projects from *Discovery Lab Crafts for Kids.*

Personalize It!

We encourage you to use *Discovery Lab Crafts for Kids* as a basis for your craft program. You, as the teacher, parent or craft leader, play an essential role in leading enjoyable and successful craft projects for your children.

Feel free to alter the craft materials and instructions to suit your children's needs. Consider what materials you have on hand, what materials are available in your area and what materials you can afford to purchase. In some cases, you may be able to substitute materials you already have for the suggested craft supplies.

In addition, don't feel confined to the crafts in a particular age-level section. You may want to adapt a craft for younger or older age levels by utilizing the simplification or enrichment ideas provided for certain crafts.

Three Steps to Success

What can you do to make sure craft time is successful and fun for your students? First, encourage creativity in each child! Remember, the process of creating is just as important as the final product. Provide a variety of materials with which children may work. Allow children to make choices on their own. Don't expect every child's project to turn out the same. Don't insist that children "stay in the lines."

Second, choose projects that are appropriate for the skill level of your students. Children become easily dis-

couraged when a project is too difficult for them. Keep your children's skill levels in mind when choosing craft projects. Finding the right projects for your students will increase the likelihood that all will be successful and satisfied with their finished products.

Finally, show an interest in the unique way each child approaches a project. Affirm the choices he or she has made. Treat each child's final product as "ingenious"!

The comments you give a child today can affect the way he or she views art in the future—so make it positive! Remember: The ability to create is part of being made in the image of God, the ultimate creator!

Crafts with a Message

Many of the projects in *Discovery Lab Crafts for Kids* can easily become crafts with a message. Children can create slogans or poetry as part of their projects; or you may want to provide photocopies of an appropriate poem, thought or Bible verse for children to attach to their crafts. Below are some examples of ways to use verses and drawings to enhance the craft projects in this book.

Be Prepared

If you are planning to use crafts with a child at home, here are three helpful tips:

- Focus on the crafts in the book designated for your child's age, but don't ignore projects that are listed for older or younger ages. Elementary-age children enjoy many of the projects geared for preschool and kindergarten children. And younger children are always interested in doing "big kid" things. Just plan on working along with the child, helping with tasks the child can't handle alone.

- Start with projects that call for materials you have around the house. Make a list of the items you do not have that are needed for projects you think your child will enjoy. Plan to gather those supplies in one expedition.

- If certain materials seem too difficult to obtain, a little thought can usually lead to appropriate substitutions. Often the homemade version ends up being an improvement over the original plan.

If you are planning to lead a group of children in doing craft projects, keep these hints in mind:

- Choose projects that will allow children to work with a variety of materials.

- Make your selection of all projects far enough in advance to allow time to gather all needed supplies in one coordinated effort. Many projects use some of the same items.

- Make up a sample of each project to be sure the directions are fully understood and potential problems can be avoided. **You may want to adapt some projects by simplifying procedures or varying the materials required.**

- Many items can be acquired as donations from people or businesses if you plan ahead and make your needs known. Many churches distribute lists of materials needed to their congregations and communities and are able to provide craft supplies at little or no cost. Some items can be brought by the children themselves.

- In making your supplies list, distinguish between items that each individual child will need and those that will be shared among a group.

- Keep in mind that some materials may be shared among more than one age level, but this works only if there is good coordination between the groups. It is extremely frustrating to a teacher to expect to have scissors, only to discover another group is using them. Basic supplies that are used repeatedly in craft projects, such as glue, scissors, felt pens, etc., should usually be provided to every group.

Craft Symbols

Many of the craft projects in *Discovery Lab Crafts for Kids* are appropriate for more than one age level. Next to the title of certain projects in this book you'll find the symbol on the left. This symbol tells which projects are suitable or adaptable for all elementary-age children—first through sixth grades. As you select projects, consider the particular children you are working with. Feel free to use your own ideas to make projects simpler or more difficult depending on the needs of your students.

In addition, some craft projects in this book require less preparation than others. The symbol shown on the right tells which projects require minimal preparation.

Lab Notes

Each craft in this book includes a very important section entitled "Lab Notes." These sections are designed to help you enhance craft times with thought-provoking conversation that is age appropriate. The "Lab Notes" section for a project may relate to an aspect of God's plan of salvation or refer to a Bible story related to the craft. Often "Lab Notes" includes interesting facts about our world, science and inventions. If your craft program includes large groups of children, you may want to share these conversation suggestions with each helper who can, in turn, use them with individuals or small groups.

GP4U Crafts

GP4U stands for "God's Plan for You." This craft section includes fun, colorful projects that will reinforce the message of God's plan of salvation for each child. A symbol represents each part of God's plan and all are used in creating these crafts. You will find an explanation of the symbols in "Do You Know About GP4U?" on page 75. In years to come, children will remember God's plan for them and how much He loves them!

(*Note:* Precut Fun Foam symbol shapes and symbol beads may be purchased from Gospel Light [in the year 2000 only] to be used for several crafts in this GP4U section.)

Helpful Hints

Using Glue with Young Children

Since preschoolers have difficulty using glue bottles effectively, you may want to try one of the following procedures. Purchase glue in large containers (up to one gallon size).

a. Pour small amounts of glue into several shallow containers (such as margarine tubs or the bottoms of soda bottles).

b. Dilute glue by mixing a little water into each container.

c. Children use paintbrushes to spread glue on their projects.

OR

a. Pour a small amount of glue into a plastic margarine tub.

b. Give each child a cotton swab. The child dips the cotton swab into the glue and rubs glue on project.

c. Excess glue can be poured back into the large container at the end of each session.

glue level   swabs

Cutting with Scissors

When cutting with scissors is required for crafts, take note of the fact that some of the children in your class may be left-handed. It is very difficult for a left-handed person to cut with scissors that were designed to be used with the right hand. Have available in your classroom two or three pairs of left-handed scissors. These can be obtained from a school supply center.

Using Acrylic Paints

Acrylic paints are required for several of the projects. Our suggestions:

• Provide smocks or old shirts for your children to wear, as acrylics may stain clothes.

• Acrylics can be expensive for a large group of children. To make paint go further, squeeze a small amount into a shallow container and add water until mixture has a creamy consistency. Or you may use acrylic house paints.

• Fill shallow containers with soapy water. Clean paintbrushes before switching colors and immediately after finishing project.

Section One
Prekindergarten—Kindergarten

Crafts for Young Children

Craft projects for young children are a blend of "I wanna do it myself!" and "I need help!" Each project, because it is intended to come out looking like a recognizable something, usually requires a certain amount of adult assistance—in preparing a pattern, in doing some cutting, in preselecting magazine pictures, in tying a knot, etc. The younger the child, the more the adult will need to do, but care must always be taken not to rob the child of the satisfaction of his or her own unique efforts. Neither must the adult's desire to have a nice finished project override the child's pleasure at experimenting with color and texture. Avoid the temptation to do the project for the child or to improve on the child's efforts.

Some of the crafts have enrichment and simplification ideas included with them. An enrichment idea provides a way to make the craft more challenging for the older child. A simplification idea helps the younger child complete the craft more successfully. If you find a child frustrated with some of the limitations of working on a structured craft—although most of the projects in this book allow plenty of leeway for children to be creative—a child's frustration may be a signal that the child needs an opportunity to work with more basic, less structured materials: blank paper and paints, play dough or abstract collages (gluing miscellaneous shapes or objects onto surfaces such as paper, cardboard or anything else to which glue will adhere). Remember the cardinal rule of thumb in any task a young child undertakes: *The process the child goes through is more important than the finished product.*

Catch-a-Comet

(10–15 MINUTES)

Materials

❏ aluminum foil
❏ narrow mylar giftwrap ribbon in a variety of colors
❏ curling ribbon in a variety of colors
For each child—
❏ one 2-inch (5-cm) Styrofoam ball

Standard Supplies

❏ pens
❏ craft glue
❏ scissors
❏ measuring stick

Preparation

Cut foil into 6-inch (15-cm) squares—one for each child. Cut curling ribbon and mylar ribbon into 2-foot (.6 m) lengths—six for each child.

Instruct each child in the following procedures:

• Choose six ribbons. With teacher's help, tie ends together in a knot (sketch a). Trim off excess above knot.
• Use pen to poke a hole in Styrofoam ball.
• Squeeze a small amount of glue into hole and insert knot of ribbon into hole of Styrofoam ball (sketch b).
• Wrap foil square around ball.

Lab Notes

(Andre), you can throw your comet way up and watch it streak through the sky. Sometimes at night we can see real comets in the sky. A comet is a huge ball of ice, rocks and dust far up in space. It looks like a fuzzy star. As it moves through space, it leaves in the sky a bright streak that looks like a tail. God made comets and lots of other things in the night sky—the moon, sun and stars.

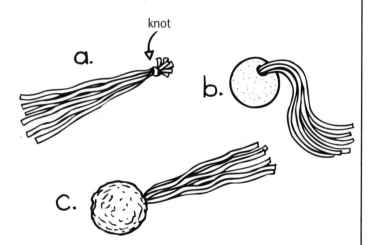

knot

a.

b.

c.

Magni-Crayon

(10–15 MINUTES)

Materials

❏ chenille wires
❏ several rolls of electrical tape
For each child—
❏ one new jumbo-sized crayon
❏ one clear plastic lid (such as Dannon yogurt lids or small delicatessen container lids)

Standard Supplies

❏ scissors
❏ hole punch
❏ ruler

Preparation

Cut chenille wires in half—one half for each child.

Instruct each child in the following procedures:

• With teacher's help, punch a hole near the edge of plastic lid.
• Thread a chenille wire through the hole and twist to secure. Then attach the lid to the flat end of crayon by twisting wires around the length of crayon (sketch a).
• With teacher's help, tightly wrap electrical tape around crayon and chenille wire, stopping at the crayon tip (sketch b). (*Note:* It is easier for children to wrap crayon while holding onto the roll.)

Enrichment Idea

Children mold several strips of aluminum foil around edge of plastic lid. Pinch and squeeze foil to secure in place.

Lab Notes

You can use your pretend magnifying glass to color pictures. Scientists use real magnifying lenses to look closely at things. What can you see through your pretend magnifying glass, (Megan)? God made lots of things for us to see. What do you like to look at that crawls? flies? buzzes? scampers?

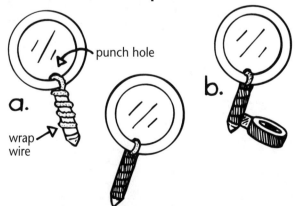

punch hole

a.

wrap wire

b.

Polished Space Rocks (10-15 MINUTES)

Materials

❏ old socks
❏ one or two blow dryers
❏ one or two extension cords

For each child—

❏ one to three smooth light-colored stones, each approximately 3 inches (7.5 cm) in diameter

Standard Supplies

❏ crayons

Preparation

Plug in blow dryers, using extension cords, if needed, to reach work area.

Instruct each child in the following procedures:

- Color your rock with crayons. Press hard to make the color dark. Color both sides.
- Lay rock on table or area where blow dryer is plugged in. Turn blow dryer on and aim at rock. Let the hot air soften the wax on the rock for about a minute (sketch a).
- Turn off blow dryer. Put an old sock over your hand. Rub the crayon markings with the sock to polish the rock (sketch b).
- Turn rock over and repeat procedure to polish rock on the opposite side.
- Color and polish additional rocks, if desired.

Lab Notes

What colors did you make your space rock, (Aria)? We can pretend your rocks came from the moon or a planet far away. Real men have been up to the moon and have brought back moon rocks. I'm glad that God made the moon to shine at night. I'm glad He made our planet, the earth, too. He made it especially for us.

a.

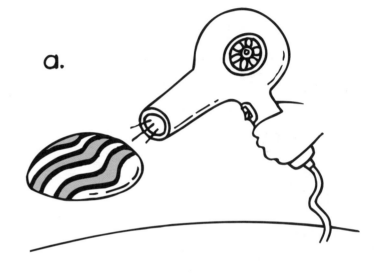

b.

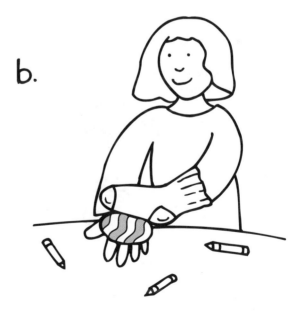

Shape Shadow Puppets (15-20 MINUTES)

<table>
<tr><td>

Materials

❏ Shape Patterns
❏ chalk in various colors
❏ flashlight
For each child—
❏ four drinking straws

</td><td>

Standard Supplies

❏ black construction paper
❏ pen
❏ glue
❏ transparent tape
❏ scissors

</td><td>

Preparation

Trace Shape Patterns onto black construction paper and cut out—one of each shape for each child.

</td></tr>
</table>

Instruct each child in the following procedures:

- With chalk, draw face on the cat and color the bird, fish and star.
- Tape one shape to the end of each straw (sketch a).
- Turn off lights. Have one person shine a flashlight against a light-colored wall. Children move shapes in front of light to create shadows on the wall (sketch b).

Enrichment Idea

Teacher or older children cut circles, triangles and squares from construction paper and children glue shapes together to create animals and objects.

Lab Notes

God made our world just right! He created the sun to keep us warm and give us light. When you go outside, the sun makes a shadow of your body on the ground. (Julia), if you jumped up and down, what do you think your shadow would do? (Jump up and down.) **What can you make your kitty shadow do on the wall?**

a.

b.

Shape Patterns

star

cat

bird

fish

"God's Love" Kaleidoscope (15-20 MINUTES)

Materials
- ❑ clear plastic wrap
- ❑ colored electrical tape
- ❑ heart-shaped stickers
- ❑ plastic confetti (preferably in transparent colors) in a variety of shapes

For each child—
- ❑ one paper towel cardboard tube
- ❑ one rubber band

Standard Supplies
- ❑ construction paper in various colors
- ❑ felt pens in various colors
- ❑ transparent tape
- ❑ glue
- ❑ scissors
- ❑ ruler

Preparation
Cut construction paper into 6x11-inch (15x27.5-cm) rectangles—one for each child. Cut plastic wrap into 4-inch (10-cm) squares—two for each child. Cover one end of each paper towel tube with one plastic wrap square by smoothing over tube end and attaching with transparent tape. Trim plastic wrap close to tape (sketch a).

Instruct each child in the following procedures:

- Decorate construction paper rectangle with felt pens and heart stickers.
- Apply glue to the back of construction paper rectangle. Then lay cardboard tube on top of glued side of paper. Wrap the paper around the tube (sketch b).
- Teacher cuts a piece of electrical tape the length of tube and helps tape the seam of paper closed.
- Stand tube on table with plastic wrap on top. Place several pieces of confetti on top of plastic.
- With teacher's help, *loosely* rubber band the second piece of plastic wrap over the confetti.
- Teacher uses a piece of electrical tape to securely tape plastic wrap edges to construction paper covering. Remove rubber band (sketch c).
- Look through kaleidoscope and turn to see the confetti move.

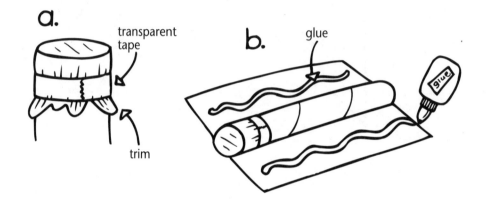

a. — transparent tape — trim

b. — glue

Lab Notes
You put heart stickers on your kaleidoscope. When we see hearts, we think of love. (Lauren), who do you love? Who loves you? God loves you, too! He sent Jesus to show how much He loves us. Our Bible says, *God...loved us and sent his Son* (1 John 4:10).

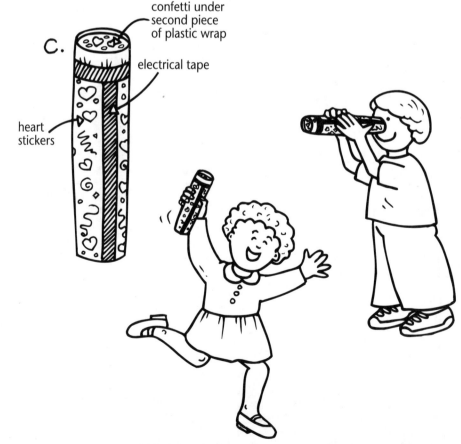

c. — confetti under second piece of plastic wrap — electrical tape — heart stickers

Nature Press (15-20 MINUTES)

Materials
- ❑ corrugated cardboard
- ❑ colored poster board
- ❑ magazines with nature pictures
- ❑ fresh flowers and leaves

For each child—
- ❑ two 4-inch (10-cm) rubber bands

Standard Supplies
- ❑ crayons or felt pens
- ❑ glue
- ❑ glue sticks
- ❑ scissors
- ❑ craft knife
- ❑ paintbrushes
- ❑ measuring stick
- ❑ shallow containers

Preparation
Cut cardboard into 6x8-inch (15x20-cm) rectangles—two for each child. Cut poster board into 6x17-inch (15x42.5-cm) rectangles—one for each child. Fold each poster board rectangle in half to make a book. On the front of each book near the top, letter "My Nature Press." Cut nature pictures from magazines for children to use for collage—five to ten small pictures for each child. Pour glue into shallow containers.

Instruct each child in the following procedures:

- On front of poster board book, glue a collage of nature pictures using a glue stick (sketch a). Glue pictures on the back of book, if desired.
- Use paintbrush to brush glue on one side of each cardboard rectangle. Cover completely with glue.
- Open the poster board book. Place one cardboard piece, glued side down, on the inside right half of poster board, making edges even (sketch b).
- Repeat with the other cardboard piece, placing it on the left half of poster board.
- Place a few flowers and/or leaves on the cardboard and then fold the book closed.
- Put two rubber bands around the press to hold it closed (sketch c).
- In a day or two, open your Nature Press to see the flowers and leaves.

a. My Nature Press

Enrichment Idea
Take children on a nature walk to collect their own leaves and flowers to press.

Lab Notes
(Sarah), what pictures did you glue to your Nature Press? Who made the plants? Who made the sky? Our Bible says, God...*made the world and everything in it* (Acts 17:24).

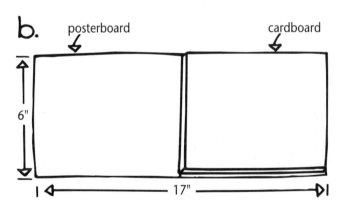

b. posterboard   cardboard

6"   17"

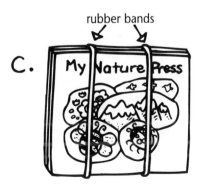

rubber bands

c. My Nature Press

Butterfly Clip (15-20 MINUTES)

Materials
- ❏ Butterfly Pattern
- ❏ flat mosaic glass or acrylic pebbles in various colors
- ❏ glitter glue pens

For each child—
- ❏ one spring-type clothespin

Standard Supplies
- ❏ photocopier
- ❏ white card stock
- ❏ crayons or felt pens
- ❏ craft glue
- ❏ scissors
- ❏ ruler

Preparation
Photocopy Butterfly Pattern onto white card stock—one for each child. Cut out butterflies. (Older children may cut out their own in class.)

Instruct each child in the following procedures

- Color both sides of butterfly with crayons or felt pens.
- With teacher's help, fold wings up on fold lines.
- Glue several pebbles along butterfly body, leaving a ½-inch (1.25-cm) space on the tail end of butterfly (sketch a).
- Glue butterfly body to the clothespin, with the tail end on the handle of clothespin (sketch b).
- Use glitter glue to make some dots and squiggles on the top of wings. Allow to dry.
- Hold onto the clothespin to make your butterfly fly!

Enrichment Idea
Glue a magnet strip to the bottom side of clothespin.

Lab Notes
Your butterflies are beautiful! (Kelley's) butterfly is (yellow with red dots). Roberto's butterfly has (black stripes). Each one of your butterflies looks different. Who made real butterflies? (God.) God made many different kinds of butterflies, too!

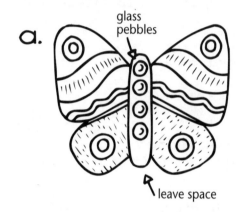

a. glass pebbles

leave space

b. glue onto clothespin

© 2000 by Gospel Light. Permission to photocopy granted. *Discovery Lab Crafts for Kids*

Butterfly Pattern

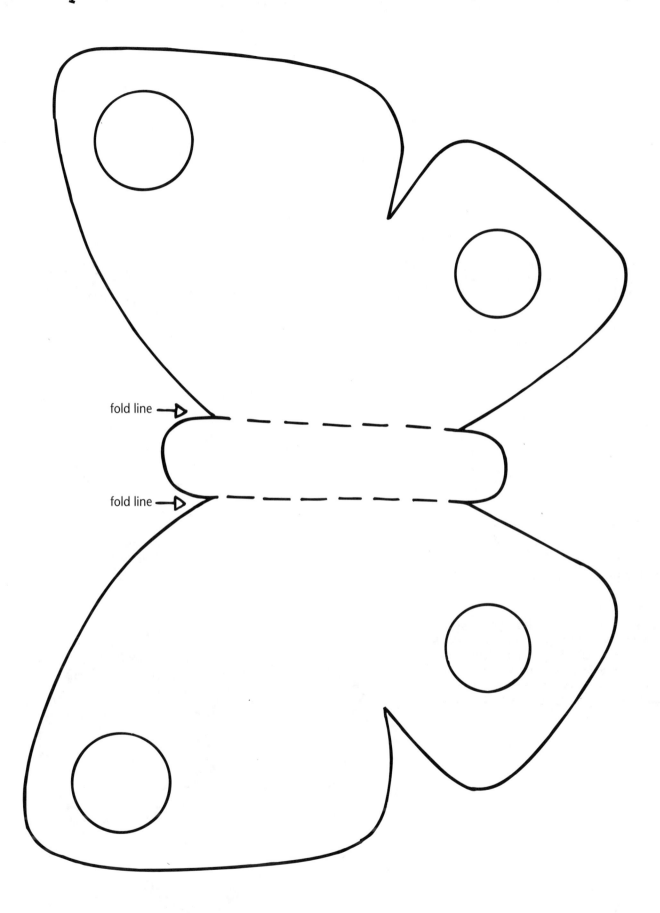

fold line →

fold line →

Loving-Heart Hanger (15-20 MINUTES)

Materials

❏ colored nylon string
❏ 18-gauge wire (available at home-improvement stores)
❏ acrylic beads in various colors and shapes
❏ colored drinking straws
❏ wire cutter

For each child—
❏ two jingle bells

Standard Supplies

❏ scissors
❏ measuring stick

Preparation

Cut wire into 36-inch (90-cm) lengths—one for each child. Cut string into 12-inch (30-cm) lengths—one for each child. Cut straws into 1-inch (2.5-cm) pieces.

Instruct each child in the following procedures:

- Thread one jingle bell onto one wire end and form a loop to hold it in place (sketch a).
- String acrylic beads and straw pieces onto wire, leaving about 6 inches (15 cm) of wire free of beads.
- Thread a second jingle bell on second wire end and form a loop to hold bell in place.
- Find center of wire and bend it to a point (sketch b).
- Bend and curve ends toward center to form a heart shape.
- With teacher's help, join wire ends together and twist wire above the bells (sketch c).
- With teacher's help, tie string length onto each side of the top of heart to make hanger.
- Adjust heart shape to hang properly.

Lab Notes

Jesus loves you and has given you people who love you, too. Our Bible says, *With love help each other* (see Galatians 5:13). **Who is someone who takes care of you? Who is someone who gives you hugs? Who is someone *you* love?**

a.

b.

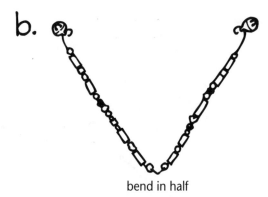

bend in half

c.

string hanger

twist wire

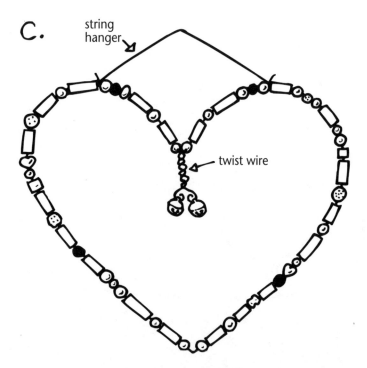

Shining-Star Soundmaker (15-20 MINUTES)

Materials
❏ star garland wire
❏ mylar ribbon
❏ iridescent star stickers
❏ dried beans

For each child—
❏ two small aluminum pie tins
❏ three jingle bells

Standard Supplies
❏ felt pen
❏ hole punch
❏ scissors
❏ stapler and staples
❏ shallow containers
❏ measuring stick

Preparation
For each pair of pie pans, punch four holes in one aluminum tin as shown in sketch a. Place a second pie tin on top and use felt pen to mark where holes are punched out; then punch holes at marks in second pie tin (sketch b). Cut some of garland wire into 18-inch (45-cm) lengths—one for each child. Cut remaining garland into 2-inch (5-cm) lengths—four for each child. Cut mylar ribbon into 4-foot (1.2-m) lengths—two for each child. Pour dried beans into shallow containers.

Instruct each child in the following procedures:

- Place one handful of dried beans into one pie tin and cover with other pie tin, lining up punched holes.
- With teacher's help, staple the two pie tins together around the edges (sketch c).
- Loosely thread long garland wire through holes in pie tins (sketch d). Twist ends together.
- With teacher's help, thread each jingle bell onto a short piece of garland wire and then attach each to a different hole in the pie tins. Twist ends to secure.
- Holding mylar ribbon, twist the fourth short wire around midpoint of ribbons. Then attach wire to the fourth hole in pie tins, twisting tightly to secure (sketch e).
- Place several star stickers on both sides of soundmaker.
- Make a sound that's "out-of-this-world" by shaking and banging your Shining-Star Soundmaker.

Simplification Idea
Omit jingle bells.

Lab Notes
Can you make a soft sound with your soundmaker, (Andy)? Now can you make a loud sound? God made us with ears so that we can hear all kinds of sounds. What are some sounds you hear right now? Listen!

a.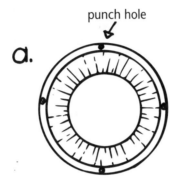
punch hole

b.

c.
staple

d.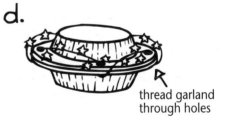
thread garland through holes

e.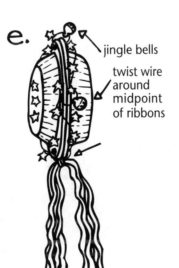
jingle bells
twist wire around midpoint of ribbons

Flying Feathered Friend (15-20 MINUTES)

Materials
❑ Bird Pattern
❑ string
❑ small colored feathers
❑ candy corn
For each child—
❑ one 12-mm jingle bell
❑ two acrylic rhinestones

Standard Supplies
❑ brightly colored card stock
❑ pencil
❑ felt pens in various colors
❑ craft glue
❑ scissors
❑ measuring stick

Preparation
Cut string into 30-inch (75-cm) lengths. Fold card stock in half, lengthwise (sketch a). Trace Bird Pattern onto card stock, placing pattern where indicated on fold—trace one bird for each child. Cut out birds. Cut a small slit in the fold on each bird where indicated by **X** on pattern.

Instruct each child in the following procedures:

- Lay bird flat and color bird with felt pens.
- With teacher's help, fold wings down and glue feathers on top of wings (sketch b).
- With teacher's help, thread string through slit in bottom of bird and tie the jingle bell onto end of string near the bottom of the bird (sketch c). Tie a loop at the top of the string to hold on to.
- Glue bird body together except for tail and wings. Bend the two sides of tail so that they stick out.
- Glue a rhinestone eye on each side of bird head.
- Glue a candy corn to each side of beak. Lay bird on its side for glue to dry.
- You can hold onto the string and run outside to make your bird fly!

Lab Notes
(Ryan), what color is your bird? What color are the feathers? God made so many different kinds of birds. He made ducks that quack, blue birds that tweet and parrots that squawk. Can you make a sound like a bird?

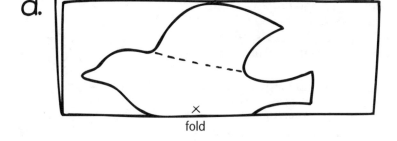

a.

fold

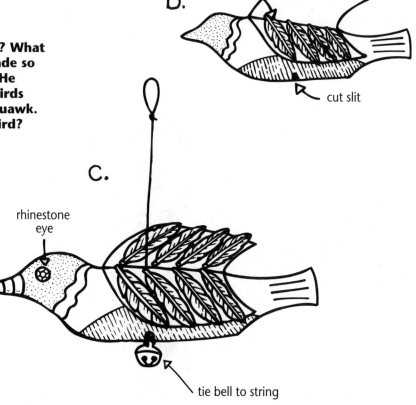

b.

glue feathers

cut slit

c.

rhinestone eye

candy corn beak

tie bell to string

Bird Pattern

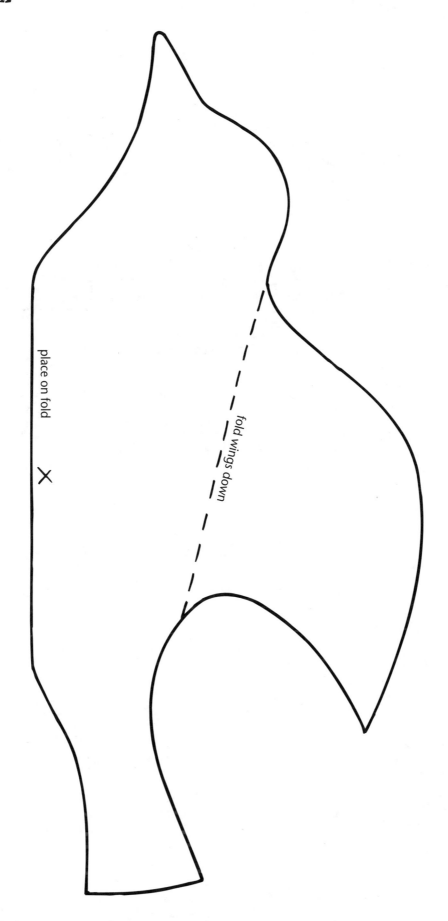

place on fold

X

fold wings down

"Adam and Eve" Picture (20-25 MINUTES)

Materials

- ❏ "Adam and Eve" Picture Pattern
- ❏ Tree Pattern
- ❏ red, yellow or orange buttons
- ❏ small flat buttons in various colors
- ❏ paper fasteners

Standard Supplies

- ❏ photocopier
- ❏ white copier paper
- ❏ 9x12-inch (22.5x30-cm) construction paper in various colors including green
- ❏ crayons
- ❏ glue sticks
- ❏ craft glue
- ❏ scissors
- ❏ hole punch

Preparation

Photocopy "Adam and Eve" Picture Pattern onto white paper—one for each child. Photocopy Tree Pattern onto green construction paper—one for each child. Cut out Tree Patterns.

Instruct each child in the following procedures:

- Rub glue stick on the back of picture along the edges and then glue picture to the center of construction paper sheet.
- Color "Adam and Eve" Picture.
- With teacher's help, punch a hole where indicated on the tree piece and on the picture.
- Place the tree piece on top of the picture, aligning holes. Push a paper fastener through the holes and secure in back of picture (sketch a).
- Use craft glue to glue red, yellow or orange buttons onto trees for fruit (sketch b).
- Glue small flat buttons onto center of flowers.
- Look in the tree to see the serpent!

Enrichment Idea

For a more durable picture, use card stock instead of copier paper.

Lab Notes

The first people God made were Adam and Eve. They were God's special friends. What happened when the snake talked to Eve in the garden? (The snake told Eve she could eat the fruit God had told them not to, so Adam and Eve ate the fruit.) **Adam and Eve disobeyed God. But God still loved them. Sometimes we do things that are wrong, too. But God still loves us, too.**

a. construction paper backing — paper fastener

b. buttons — buttons

Tree Pattern

"Adam and Eve" Picture Pattern

Adam and Eve

"Jesus Calms the Storm" Picture (20-25 MINUTES)

Materials
- ❏ Jesus, Boat and Sail Patterns
- ❏ 9x12-inch (22.5x30-cm) Fun Foam sheets in black, blue, brown and yellow (available at craft stores)
- ❏ cotton balls
- ❏ brown chenille wires

For each child—
- ❏ one craft stick
- ❏ one paper fastener

Standard Supplies
- ❏ photocopier
- ❏ white card stock
- ❏ pen
- ❏ felt pens in various colors including black
- ❏ craft glue
- ❏ scissors
- ❏ ruler

Preparation
Cut blue and black foam sheets in half—one half of each color for each child. Cut one long edge of blue foam half-sheets to look like waves (sketch a). Fold in half, short sides together. Starting at fold, make a cut 2½ inches (6.25 cm) long and 2 inches (5 cm) down from wavy edge. Open foam sheet. You should have a 5-inch (12.5-cm) slit across the middle. Squeeze a line of glue along the edges of black foam where indicated in Sketch b. Place wavy edge of blue foam on top of glue, keeping the edge of slit below the edge of black foam. Trace Boat Pattern onto brown Fun Foam and Sail Pattern onto yellow Fun Foam—one of each for each child. Cut out. Cut chenille wires into 3-inch (7.5-cm) lengths—one for each child. Photocopy Jesus Pattern onto white card stock—one for each child.

Instruct each child in the following procedures:

- With a black felt pen, draw lines across the boat to make boards.
- With teacher's help, place the boat near the left side of picture, tucked under the wave piece about ¼ inch (.625 cm), so the waves are in front of boat. Push a paper fastener through the boat and black background to secure boat to picture (sketch c).
- Glue the sail to the black background, slightly above boat.
- Glue the chenille wire to the center of sail to make a mast.
- Lightly color several cotton balls with black felt pen to make stormy clouds. Glue cotton balls to the black sky.
- Color Jesus figure with felt pens. Cut out or have teacher cut out.
- Glue a craft stick to the back of Jesus figure (sketch d).
- Allow glue to dry on picture and Jesus figure.
- Place Jesus in the sea to walk on the water (sketch e). Make the boat rock back and forth in the storm.

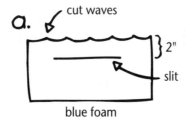

a.
cut waves
2"
slit
blue foam

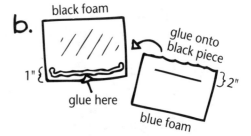

b.
black foam
glue onto black piece
1"
glue here
blue foam
2"

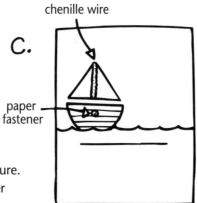

c.
chenille wire
paper fastener

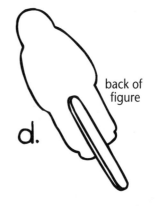

d.
back of figure

e.

Simplification Ideas
Eliminate drawing on boat and coloring clouds with felt pen. Use sheets of construction paper or colored card stock instead of Fun Foam.

Lab Notes
Jesus took care of His friends when they were afraid in the storm. Jesus is so powerful that He told the wind and the waves to stop. The sea became very still. Jesus will take care of us, too. When is a time you have been afraid, (Nicole)? When you are afraid, you can ask Jesus to take care of you.

Jesus, Boat and Sail Patterns

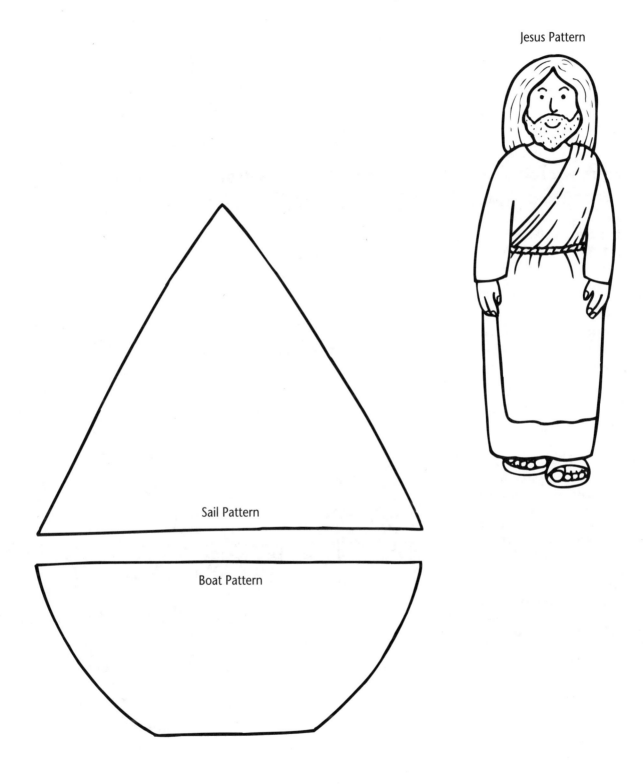

Jesus Pattern

Sail Pattern

Boat Pattern

Fingerprint Flowers (20-25 MINUTES)

Materials
- ❑ washable ink pads in two or three colors
- ❑ ribbon
- ❑ bamboo garden stakes
- ❑ hand saw

Standard Supplies
- ❑ colored card stock
- ❑ yellow construction paper
- ❑ pencil
- ❑ glue
- ❑ transparent tape
- ❑ scissors
- ❑ measuring stick
- ❑ water and soap for cleanup

Preparation
Use saw to cut bamboo garden stakes into 12-inch (30-cm) long sticks—three to five sticks for each child. Draw 6-inch (15-cm) flower shapes on card stock and cut out—three to five for each child (sketch a). Draw 3-inch (7.5-cm) circles on construction paper for flower centers and cut out—three to five for each child. Cut ribbon into 18-inch (45-cm) lengths—one for each child.

Instruct each child in the following procedures:

- Glue round centers to flowers.
- Press your finger on an ink pad and then press on flower to decorate. You can make fingerprints all around the flower edge or only in the middle (sketch b).
- Make fingerprints on remaining flowers. Wash hands.
- Attach bamboo sticks to back of flowers with tape (sketch c).
- With teacher's help, tie "bouquet" of flowers with ribbon (sketch d).
- You may give a flower to someone to show your love!

Lab Notes
(Karina), you may give a flower to someone you love. Who is someone you love? (Child responds.) **Who is someone who loves you?** (Child responds.) **God loves you, too. Our Bible says, God...loved us and sent his Son** (1 John 4:10). **Jesus came to show His love for us and to teach us how to love each other.**

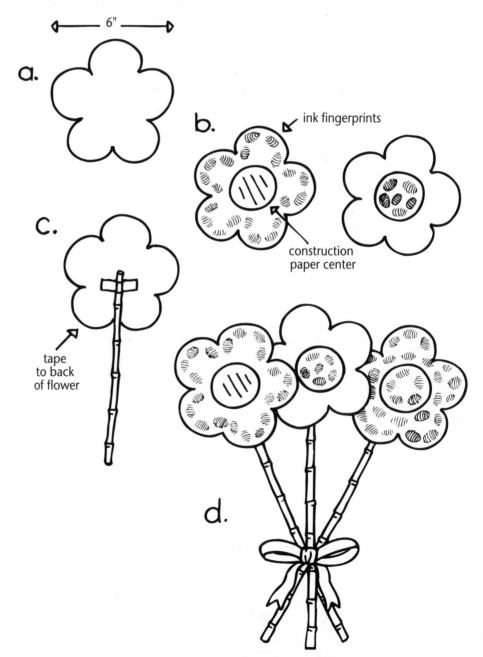

a. ← 6" →

b. ink fingerprints

construction paper center

c. tape to back of flower

d.

"Comet the Cat" Paper Plate Puppet (20-30 MINUTES)

Materials

❏ thick yellow and/or orange yarn
❏ black permanent felt pens

For each child—

❏ one 9-inch (22.5-cm) yellow or orange paper plate
❏ one 2½-inch (6.25-cm) rubber band
❏ two paper fasteners
❏ two large wiggle eyes
❏ one toilet paper tube
❏ one yellow or orange chenille wire

Standard Supplies

❏ yellow or orange construction paper
❏ pencil
❏ glue
❏ hot glue gun and glue sticks
❏ scissors
❏ measuring stick

Preparation

Cut yarn into 18-inch (45-cm) lengths—one for each child. Cut remaining yarn into 2-inch (5-cm) pieces—at least eight pieces for each child. Cut each chenille wire into six 2-inch (5-cm) pieces. Cut construction paper into 4 1/2x6-inch (11.25x15-cm) rectangles—one for each child. From remaining construction paper, cut small triangles for cat's ears—two for each child. Plug in glue gun out of reach of children.

Instruct each child in the following procedures:

- Spread glue on construction paper rectangle and wrap around paper tube (sketch a). Set aside.
- Glue wiggle eyes to the colored side (top) of plate.
- With felt pen, draw cat's nose below eyes (sketch b).
- For cat whiskers, glue three chenille wire pieces on either side of nose.
- For cat's ears, glue construction paper triangles to top edge of plate.
- For cat fur, glue short pieces of yarn around paper plate rim.
- With teacher's help, push two paper fasteners about 3 inches (7.5 cm) apart underneath the cat's nose and whiskers in the paper plate (sketch b). Open prongs in back of plate.
- With teacher's help, place a rubber band around paper fasteners.
- On opposite sides of covered paper tube, teacher cuts 1-inch (2.5-cm) slits at top of tube (sketch c).
- Insert bottom edge of plate into slits cut in tube, properly aligning face.
- Teacher uses hot glue to secure paper plate in slits.
- Tie 18-inch (45-cm) length of yarn to lower "lip" of rubber band (sketch d).
- Run yarn through the center of the tube.
- Hold onto paper tube and pull yarn to move mouth.

Simplification Idea

Instead of cardboard tube attachment, teacher glues a tongue depressor to plate for handle. Children move mouth with their fingers.

Lab Notes

(Kristen), what sound does a cat make? (Meow.) **You can use your cat puppet to tell stories or entertain your brother, sister or friends. What was the story from the Bible we heard today?**

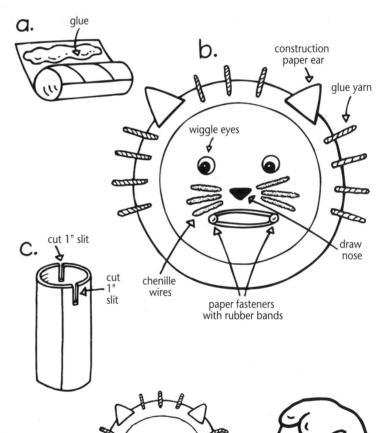

a. glue

b. construction paper ear / glue yarn / wiggle eyes / draw nose / chenille wires / paper fasteners with rubber bands

c. cut 1" slit / cut 1" slit

d. tie yarn and thread through tube / pull on string to make cat talk

Sunny-Sky Mobile (25-30 MINUTES)

Materials
- ❏ Sun Face Pattern
- ❏ yellow and orange crepe paper streamers
- ❏ tempera paints in rainbow colors
- ❏ table salt in shakers
- ❏ cotton balls
- ❏ nail or craft needle
- ❏ string

For each child—
- ❏ two 9-inch (22.5-cm) yellow paper plates

Standard Supplies
- ❏ photocopier
- ❏ yellow or orange card stock
- ❏ craft glue
- ❏ transparent tape
- ❏ scissors
- ❏ stapler and staples
- ❏ paintbrushes
- ❏ measuring stick
- ❏ shallow containers
- ❏ newspaper

Preparation
Photocopy Sun Face Pattern onto yellow or orange card stock—one for each child. Cut streamers into 12-inch (30-cm) lengths—14 for each child. Cut string into 24-inch (60-cm) lengths—one for each child. With nail or craft needle, poke a small hole in center of half the paper plates. Cut the remaining paper plates in half and then cut out the centers, leaving the curved rims (sketch a)—two halves for each child. Pour paints into shallow containers. Cover work area with newspaper.

Instruct each child in the following procedures:

- Paint both paper plate halves to look like rainbows on the white (bottom) sides (sketch b).
- Sprinkle with table salt. Set aside to dry.
- Cut out Sun Face.
- With teacher's help, push string length through the hole in the uncut plate. Tape the string end to the yellow (top) side of plate (sketch c).
- Glue the Sun Face to the yellow side of paper plate, covering the taped string.
- Lay the paper plate face side down. Glue ends of streamers around the edge of plate, overlapping them to make sun's rays (sketch d).
- Glue one or two cotton balls to each end of each painted rainbow.
- With teacher's help, staple both sides of rainbow together, painted sides out, with the string in the middle and about 8 inches (20 cm) above sun (sketch e).
- Hang the sun above your head and look up to see the sun smiling at you (sketch f)! Watch the sun's rays flutter in the breeze.

Simplification Ideas
For younger children, draw lines to define color rows on plates used for rainbow. Eliminate paint and salt and have children color rainbow with felt pens.

Lab Notes
(Evan), I saw you helping (Sasha) glue her streamers on her sun. You were being kind and loving to her. Jesus wants us to show love to others. Our Bible says, *With love help each other* (see Galatians 5:13). **How do you show love to your (sister, dad, friend, etc.)?**

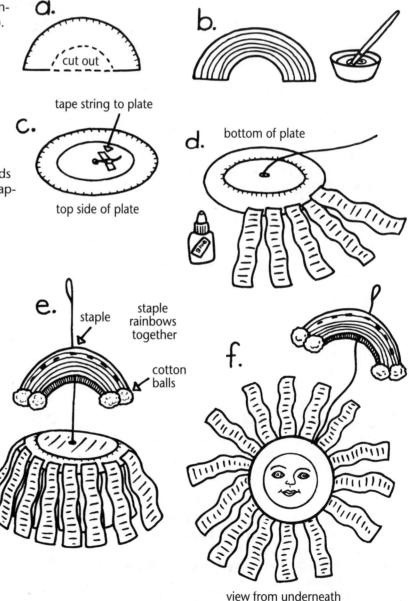

a.
cut out

b.
tape string to plate

c.
top side of plate

d.
bottom of plate

e.
staple
staple rainbows together
cotton balls

f.
view from underneath

Sun Face Pattern

Computer Bug (25-30 MINUTES)

Materials

- ❏ Fun Foam sheets (available at craft stores) or mat board
- ❏ gray acrylic paint

For each child—
- ❏ two small round magnets
- ❏ one small box (such as cake mix or baby cereal box)
- ❏ one glitter pom-pom
- ❏ two small wiggle eyes
- ❏ one tongue depressor

Standard Supplies

- ❏ light blue or gray construction paper
- ❏ felt pen
- ❏ glue sticks
- ❏ transparent tape
- ❏ craft glue
- ❏ craft knife
- ❏ paintbrushes
- ❏ ruler
- ❏ shallow containers
- ❏ newspaper

Preparation

Use craft knife to cut out one long side from each box (sketch a). Tape closed any sides of box that are opened. Cut Fun Foam or mat board into 6x8-inch (15x20-cm) rectangles—one for each child. Then use craft knife to cut a 4x6-inch (10x15-cm) rectangle out of each rectangle to make a frame (sketch b). Cut construction paper into 5½x7½-inch (13.75x 18.75-cm) rectangles—one for each child. Pour paint into shallow containers. Cover work area with newspaper.

Instruct each child in the following procedures:

- Paint the three narrow sides of box with gray paint.
- Glue one magnet onto end of tongue depressor.
- With teacher's help, glue wiggle eyes onto pom-pom.
- Glue pom-pom onto other magnet (sketch c). Allow glue to dry.
- Teacher writes "Jesus Loves (name of child)" on construction paper rectangle. (Older children may write their own names.)
- Use glue sticks to glue back of construction paper to front of box (sketch a).
- Squeeze glue along edges of construction paper and glue frame in place (sketch d).
- Place magnetic bug on top of box. Hold tongue depressor inside box with the magnet side up. Move tongue depressor back and forth and watch your computer bug roam around the screen!

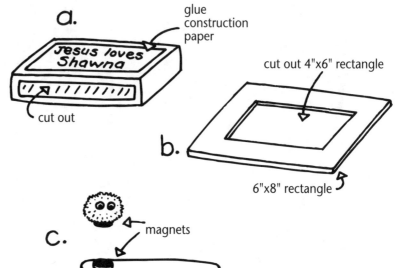

Simplification Ideas

Eliminate painting boxes. Use pre-cut photo mats.

Enrichment Ideas

Glue on small geometric Fun Foam shapes or apply stickers to decorate frame.

Lab Notes

(Shawna), what does your computer screen say? (Jesus loves [Shawna].) **God sent Jesus to show His love to people. What did Jesus do that showed love?** (He helped people. He made them well. He was their friend.) **How can you show love to people?**

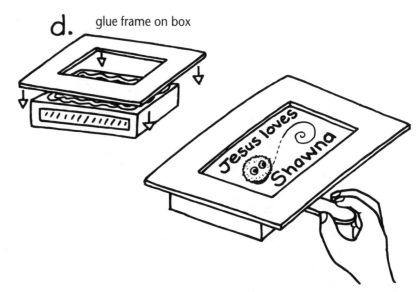

Section Two
Grades 1–3

Crafts for Younger Elementary

Children in the first few years of school delight in completing craft projects. They have a handle on most of the basic skills needed, they are eager to participate and their taste in art has usually not yet surpassed their ability to produce. In other words, they generally like the things they make.

Since reading ability is not a factor in most craft projects, crafts can be a great leveler among a group. Some children excel here who may or may not be top achievers in other areas.

You may find additional projects suitable for younger elementary children in the first section of this book—"Crafts for Young Children."

Crystal Cross (10–15 MINUTES)

Materials

❏ borax
❏ measuring spoons
❏ plastic spoons
❏ yarn or string
❏ permanent felt pen
❏ stove
❏ saucepan
❏ several thermoses or insulated carafes

For each child—
❏ one 16-oz. disposable plastic cup
❏ one purple chenille wire
❏ one long pencil

Standard Supplies

❏ scissors
❏ measuring stick
❏ water
❏ paper towels

Preparation

Cut yarn or string into 18-inch (45-cm) lengths—one for each child. Heat water in saucepan on stove—1½-2 cups for each child. Pour into thermoses or insulated carafes.

Instruct each child in the following procedures:

- Bend the chenille wire into an outline of a cross shape. Twist ends together to close shape and press twisted ends flat (sketch a).
- Tie one end of yarn or string to top of cross.
- With felt pen, write your name on plastic cup.
- Use measuring spoon to place three tablespoons of borax into plastic cup.
- With teacher's help, pour hot water into the cup until there is about 1 inch (2.5 cm) of space from the top. Stir gently with spoon to mix solution.
- Hold onto the yarn or string tied to cross and lower cross into the borax solution. Make sure chenille wire is completely covered with water.
- Wrap the yarn or string around a pencil and set the pencil across the top of cup (sketch b).
- Teacher places cup where it will set overnight.
- On the following day, carefully remove your cross from the cup. It will be covered with crystals!
- Unwind yarn or string from the pencil. Allow cross to dry on paper towels; then take home and hang up in a window.

Simplification Idea

Younger children may make a cross by twisting two small pieces of chenille wire together.

Enrichment Ideas

Children may make a variety of shapes with differently colored chenille wires (heart, star, flower, geometric, etc.) and use to make mobiles (see GP4U Disc Mobile, p. 78).

Lab Notes

As the water and borax solution cools, the borax molecules rearrange themselves and stack together to form crystals. Your Crystal Cross can remind you that when Jesus died on the cross, He rearranged everything. Before, sin kept us apart from God. But since Jesus took the punishment for our sin, now anyone who believes in Him can be a part of God's family!

a.

press twisted ends flat

b.

Totally Tubular Necklace (10–15 MINUTES)

Materials
- ¼-inch (.625-cm) clear vinyl tubing (available at home-improvement stores)
- metallic chenille wires
- seed beads
- plastic confetti

For each child—
- two ½-inch (1.25-cm) round magnets
- one colored wood barrel bead (with large hole)

Standard Supplies
- low-temperature glue gun and glue sticks
- scissors
- measuring stick
- shallow containers

Preparation
Cut tubing into 20-inch (50-cm) lengths—one for each child. Place seed beads and confetti in separate containers. Plug in glue gun out of reach of children.

Instruct each child in the following procedures:

- Insert seed beads and confetti into tubing to decorate necklace. Use chenille wires to push items through tube (sketch a).
- Insert chenille wires into tube to decorate necklace. Cut wires into shorter pieces, if desired.
- Thread one large barrel bead onto tubing (sketch b).
- Attach two magnets to each other. With teacher's help, use glue gun to attach the outer sides of magnets to the ends of plastic tube (sketch c). Allow glue to harden.
- To wear your Tubular Necklace, pull magnets apart, put necklace around your neck and reconnect magnets in back.

Lab Notes
When you turn the magnets the right way, what happens? (They stick together.) **What happens when you try to put the wrong sides of magnets together?** (They won't connect.) **The same thing happened when Adam and Eve sinned. At first, Adam and Eve were connected to God. They loved God and talked with Him every day. But when they turned away from God and chose to do wrong, they couldn't be close to God anymore. But God had a plan to send Jesus so that everyone can be close to Him again. Now God will forgive us when we do something wrong, if we tell Him we are sorry. Then it's like turning the magnets around so that they connect—we can stick to God forever!**

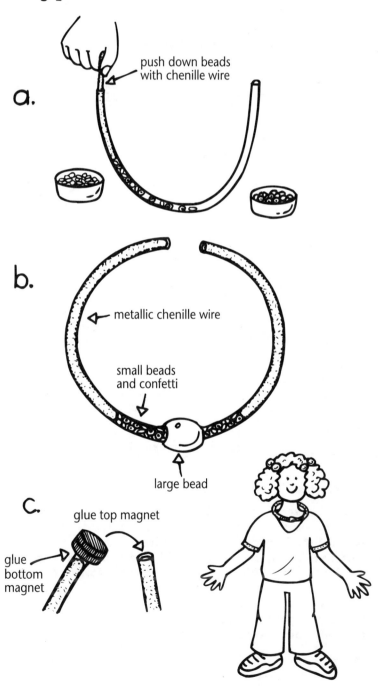

a. push down beads with chenille wire

b. metallic chenille wire / small beads and confetti / large bead

c. glue top magnet / glue bottom magnet

Seed Science Pendant (10–15 MINUTES)

Materials

❏ colored plastic lanyard or thin ribbon
❏ hand or power drill
❏ drill bit (same size as eye screws used)
❏ cotton balls
❏ pony beads

For each child—
❏ two large seeds (sunflower, bean, etc.)
❏ one eye screw
❏ one small clear plastic container with lid
  (bead container, glitter container, film
  canister), at least 1 inch (2.5 cm) in diameter

Optional—
❏ hammer
❏ nail (same size as eye screws used)

Standard Supplies

❏ scissors
❏ measuring stick
❏ water
❏ one or two shallow
  containers

Preparation

Drill a hole in the center of each lid. (*Optional:* If lids are made of flexible plastic, such as film canister lids, you may be able to use a thin nail to make holes.) Cut lanyard or ribbon into 30-inch (75-cm) lengths—one for each child. Fill shallow containers with water.

Instruct each child in the following procedures:

- Screw eye screw through hole in lid.
- Moisten one or two cotton balls with water and place in the small plastic container.
- Place two seeds in with the cotton balls. Make sure each seed is on a moist portion of a cotton ball. Place lid on the container (sketch a).
- Thread the lanyard through the eye screw.
- Thread a few beads on either side of eye screw, if desired. Then pull lanyard ends even and tie together in a knot (sketch b). Trim ends.
- Wear your Seed Science Pendant around your neck when you're outside or hang it in a bright place indoors where you can watch it. Add a teaspoon of water, if needed, to keep moist. In a few days your seeds will sprout. Watch them grow!

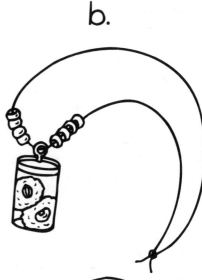

a.   eye screw

seeds

cotton balls

b.

Enrichment Idea

Children decorate clay pots with acrylic paint. Later at home, they transplant their sprouted seed(s) into the painted pots.

Lab Notes

When your seedlings are about 2 inches (5 cm) long, carefully remove them from the container and plant them in dirt. God made our earth just right for things to live and grow. What did God create to help your plants grow? (Water. Sun. Earth.) **Don't forget to water your new plants once you've put them outside! After you've transplanted your seeds, you can sprout new seeds in your pendant—just add new cotton balls, water and seeds.**

Starry-Sky Window Ornament (10—15 MINUTES)

Materials
❏ star garland wire
❏ star plastic confetti
❏ glitter
❏ blue food coloring
For each child—
❏ one small margarine lid
❏ one 6-oz. disposable cup
❏ craft stick
❏ one Post-It Note

Standard Supplies
❏ pens
❏ glue
❏ scissors
❏ ruler

Preparation
Cut garland wire into 2-inch (5-cm) lengths—one for each child.

Instruct each child in the following procedures:

- Cut Post-It Note into four strips, with each strip containing a sticky portion. On the sticky side of each strip, write one number (1 through 4) on the nonsticky end.
- Turn plastic lid upside down. Stick the Post-It Note strips on bottom of lid so that numbers extend from edge of circle (sketch a).
- Fill cup half full with glue.
- Use craft stick to mix two or three drops of food coloring into the glue. Stir until color is well blended.
- Carefully pour glue mixture into plastic lid.
- Bend wire garland into a loop and twist ends together. Pull off any large stars from garland. Place twisted ends of loop into glue (sketch b).
- Place star confetti and large stars from garland into glue mixture.
- Sprinkle glitter onto glue mixture.
- Allow glue to dry for at least four days (at home or at VBS). Keep track of days by pulling off one numbered strip for each day. On the fourth day, carefully remove dried glue ornament from the lid. Hang in front of a window to see your starry sky.

Lab Notes
On the fourth day of creation, God created the sun, moon and stars. What other things did God create? What is God's best creation? (People.) **God made people so that He could love us and so that we can love Him.**

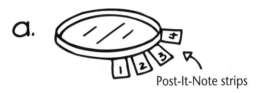

a.

Post-It-Note strips

b.

Not a Cordless Phone! (20–25 MINUTES)

Materials
- ❏ brightly colored heavy paper napkins or tissue paper
- ❏ string
- ❏ hand or power drill
- ❏ 1/16-inch (.156-cm) drill bit

For each child—
- ❏ two 10-oz. clear plastic cups

Standard Supplies
- ❏ white glue
- ❏ scissors
- ❏ sponge brushes
- ❏ measuring stick
- ❏ shallow containers
- ❏ water

Preparation
Cut string into 20-foot (6-m) lengths—one for each child. Drill a hole in the center of the bottom of each cup. Cut the napkins or tissue paper into 1-inch (2.5-cm) squares. Pour glue into shallow containers and thin with water.

Instruct each child in the following procedures:

- Thread one end of string through the bottom of one cup. Make a large knot that won't pull out of the hole. Repeat with the other cup (sketch a).
- With sponge brush, brush a thin layer of glue onto a section of the inside of one cup.
- Lay napkin or tissue paper squares over the glue in an interesting pattern. Then lightly dab a thin layer of glue on top of squares (sketch b).
- Continue to apply squares to the rest of the inside surface of cup. Then repeat with the remaining cup. Allow to dry thoroughly.
- To use the phone, have a friend stand far enough away so that the string is tight and hold one cup to his or her ear while you talk slowly into your cup (sketch c). Make sure the string isn't touching anything (like furniture or a wall) or your telephone will get disconnected!

a.

large knot

b.

c.

Lab Notes
Your telephone works because the sound vibrations from your voice travel through the string. The other cup amplifies the sound and collects it so that someone else can hear it. If something touches the string, it stops the flow of vibrations. Your phone will be "disconnected."

    Jesus came to earth as a way to connect us to God. When people choose to do wrong things, their sin causes a separation from God. So Jesus came to take the punishment for our sin. Because He died on the cross and rose again, we can be connected to God and become a part of His family.

Lab-Notes Clipboard (20–25 MINUTES)

Materials
- black Fun Foam (available at craft stores)
- heavy cardboard
- nylon string in bright colors
- brightly colored poster board
- black permanent felt pen
- clear transparencies or plastic lids

For each child—
- one spring-type clothespin
- one new pencil, sharpened

Standard Supplies
- copier paper
- lightweight cardboard
- felt pens in various colors
- craft glue
- scissors
- hole punch
- craft knife
- measuring stick

Preparation
Cut heavy cardboard and poster board into 6x9-inch (15x22.5-cm) rectangles—one of each for each child. Cut lightweight cardboard into several 2-inch (5-cm) diameter circle patterns. Cut string into 24-inch (60-cm) lengths. Cut black Fun Foam into ½-inch (1.25-cm) wide strips that are the same length as clothespins—one for each child. Cut copier paper in half widthwise—two or three half-sheets for each child.

Instruct each child in the following procedures:

- Set a circle pattern on the clear transparency or plastic lid. Use permanent felt pen to trace around the pattern to make a circle. Cut out circle. This is the "magnifying glass lens."
- Place a dot of glue at the clip end of clothes pin. Place edge of plastic "lens" on top of glue (sketch a).
- For magnifying glass handle, glue the black Fun Foam strip over the clothespin. Set aside to dry.
- Glue poster board rectangle to cardboard rectangle, making sure edges and corners are glued down.
- With teacher's help, use hole punch to punch a hole in one top corner of board.
- Tie one end of the string through the hole and knot to secure. Tie the other end of string to the eraser end of pencil (sketch b).
- Use felt pens to write the words "Jesus Came to Show God's Love" on the poster board. Then draw a picture and/or designs (sketch c).
- You may attach a few half-sheets of paper to your clipboard by clipping the magnifying glass clothespin to the top edge of board.
- Place the pencil in the clothespin handle to hold onto clipboard (sketch d).

Simplification Idea
Teacher writes or types "Jesus Came to Show God's Love" on paper and photocopies—one for each child. Child cuts out and glues to poster board.

Lab Notes
God sent Jesus to our world to show us what God is like. What are some things Jesus did that showed love? What are some things He did that showed that God is powerful?

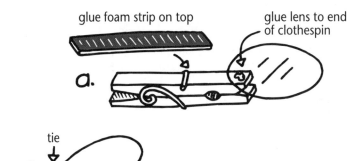

glue foam strip on top · glue lens to end of clothespin

a.

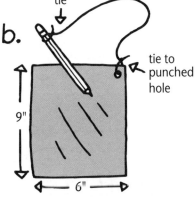

tie · tie to punched hole

b. · 9" · 6"

c. · Jesus Came to Show God's Love

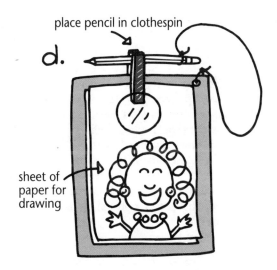

place pencil in clothespin

d.

sheet of paper for drawing

Spectacular Spectacles (20–25 MINUTES)

Materials
- ❏ Spectacles Patterns
- ❏ clear and colored cellophane
- ❏ sequin bangles in a variety of shapes (star, flower, etc.)
- ❏ elastic cording

For each child—
- ❏ one brown paper lunch bag
- ❏ two sets of Velcro rounds

Standard Supplies
- ❏ photocopier
- ❏ brightly colored card stock
- ❏ glue
- ❏ scissors
- ❏ hole punch
- ❏ ruler

Preparation
Cut elastic cording into 12-inch (30-cm) lengths—one for each child. Photocopy Spectacles Patterns onto card stock—set of two for each child. Cut cellophane into 6½-x1½-inch (16.25x3.75-cm) rectangles—one clear and one colored rectangle for each child.

Instruct each child in the following procedures:

- Cut out spectacles. With teacher's help, cut out eye holes.
- Glue the clear cellophane rectangle over eye holes on one pair of spectacles (sketch a).
- Glue the colored cellophane rectangle over eye holes on the other pair of spectacles.
- Glue sequins on front of both spectacle frames to decorate.
- Make sure both sides of Velcro rounds are attached together. Remove the backing from Velcro rounds and stick one round to each top front corner of glasses with clear lenses (sketch b).
- Lay the spectacles with colored lenses, decorated side up, on top of the clear lenses, lining up glasses evenly. Press to attach the remaining sticky side of Velcro rounds (sketch c). Pull off colored spectacles. One side of each Velcro round will now be attached to the colored spectacles.
- Punch a hole on both sides of the clear spectacles.
- Thread one end of elastic cord through each hole. Tie and knot elastic to each side of glasses (sketch d). Trim ends.
- Look through the clear lenses. Then attach the colored lenses.

a.
glue cellophane over eye holes
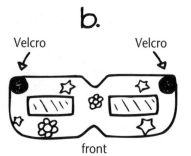
back

b.
Velcro   Velcro

front

c.
colored cellophane   press together
clear cellophane
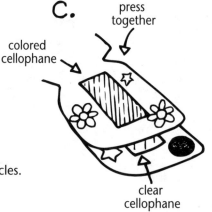

colored lenses
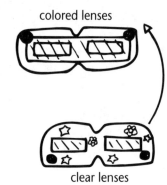
clear lenses

d.
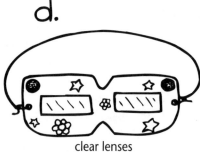
clear lenses

Lab Notes
What color is everything when you look through your colored spectacles, (Justin)? What colors do you see when you look through the clear spectacles? (All colors.) **Light contains colors that we can't see. You can see colors in light when you look at a rainbow. The drops of water in the sky allow us to see the colors in light. God made our eyes to see many different colors! What is your favorite color?**

Spectacles Patterns

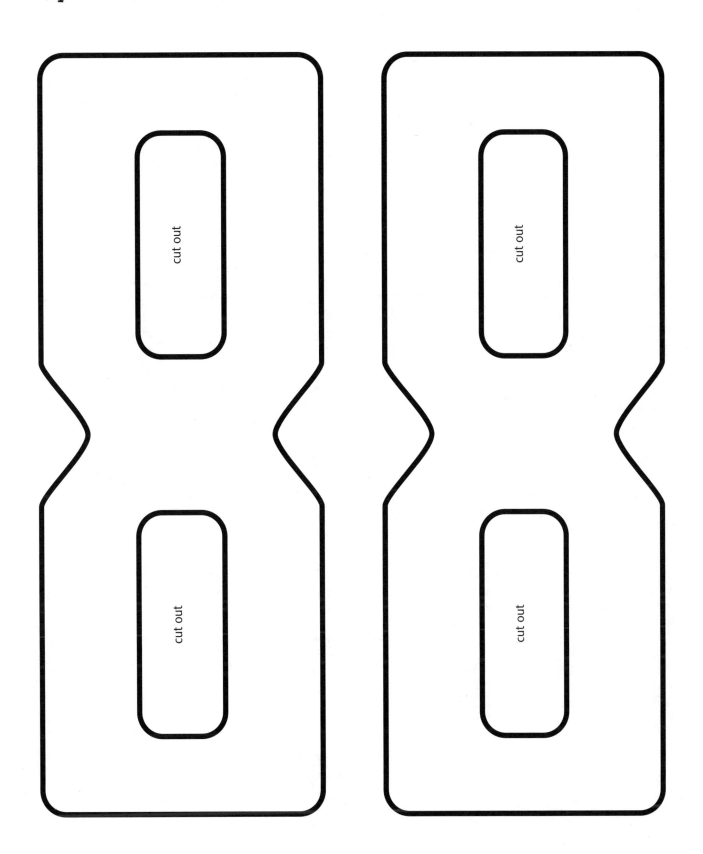

cut out

cut out

cut out

cut out

"Time to Know" Book (25–30 MINUTES)

Materials
- ❑ white and red poster board
- ❑ plastic bubble wrap
- ❑ acrylic paint in silver or other metallic colors
- ❑ black permanent felt pens
- ❑ disposable plastic plates

For each child—
- ❑ old computer or music CD
- ❑ one paper fastener

Standard Supplies
- ❑ felt pens in various colors including red
- ❑ craft glue
- ❑ scissors
- ❑ hole punch
- ❑ measuring stick
- ❑ newspaper

Preparation
Cut white poster board into 11x14-inch (27.5x35-cm) rectangles—one for each child; fold each rectangle in half to form a book. Cut red poster board into ½-inch wide (1.25-cm) strips; then cut strips into 1½-inch (3.75-cm) and 2-inch (5-cm) lengths—one of each for each child. Cut bubble wrap into 5-inch (12.5-cm) squares—one for each child. Cover work area with newspaper. Pour paint onto disposable plates.

Instruct each child in the following procedures:

- With felt pen, letter "Time to Know" on the front cover of book (sketch a).
- On the inside left side of book, use felt pens to draw a heart in the center of page.
- Draw a picture of Jesus above the heart. Then write your name below the heart (sketch b).
- At the top of right side of book, write "all the time."
- To make a clock for your book, use black permanent felt pen to write the numbers of a clock (1 through 12) on the unprinted side of CD (sketch c).
- Glue the back of clock under the lettered words on the right side of book (sketch d).
- Snip one end of each red poster board strip into a point to make clock hands (sketch e).
- With hole punch, punch holes in the square ends of clock hands; then push paper fastener through the holes and through the center of CD, making a hole in the poster board (sketch f). Secure fastener in back of book by bending ends flat against poster board.
- Lay book with cover side up.
- Lay bubble wrap square in paint and then press onto front and back covers to decorate book. Don't paint over lettered words. Allow paint to dry.

Lab Notes

What does your book say? (Jesus loves [Katrina] all the time.) **We know that Jesus loves us because the Bible tells us so. What can you remember from our story today that shows that Jesus loves us?** (He died to forgive the wrong things we do.)

a.

b.

c.

d. glue clock

e. snip ends to make points

f. insert paper fastener

hole

38

© 2000 by Gospel Light. Permission to photocopy granted. *Discovery Lab Crafts for Kids*

"God Made the World" Picture (25—30 MINUTES)

Materials
- ❏ black poster board—one sheet for every four children
- ❏ blue and green acrylic paint
- ❏ glow-in-the-dark star stickers
- ❏ brightly colored nylon string
- ❏ serrated knife

For every two children—
- ❏ one 3-inch (7.5-cm) Styrofoam ball

Standard Supplies
- ❏ bright colored paper
- ❏ felt pens
- ❏ pastel-colored crayons
- ❏ craft glue
- ❏ hole punch
- ❏ scissors
- ❏ paintbrushes
- ❏ measuring stick
- ❏ shallow containers
- ❏ newspaper

Preparation
Use knife to cut Styrofoam balls in half. Cut each poster board sheet into fourths—one fourth for each child. Punch two holes in one long side of each poster board, each hole 2 inches (5 cm) in from end and ½-inch (1.25 cm) down from top (sketch a). Cut string into 16-inch (40-cm) lengths. Cut paper into 2x8-inch (5x20-cm) strips—one for each child. Pour paints into separate shallow containers. Cover work area with newspaper.

Instruct each child in the following procedures:

- Set the Styrofoam ball half in the center of poster board and trace around it with a crayon (sketch a). Remove the Styrofoam ball.
- Paint Styrofoam ball to look like the earth, using blue paint for the ocean and green paint for the land. Set aside to dry.
- With felt pen, write "God made the world" on the paper strip and glue to poster board below the traced circle (sketch a).
- Use crayons to draw moon, sun and planets in space. Don't draw inside the traced circle.
- Attach glow-in-the-dark star stickers to picture.
- Glue Styrofoam earth onto traced circle on picture (sketch b).
- Push string through holes and tie a knot at each end for hanging. Trim ends if needed.

Enrichment Ideas
Purchase glow-in-the-dark paint for children to use to paint moon, sun and planets. Use a half sheet of poster board to make larger pictures.

Lab Notes
You can hang your picture on the wall in your room. When you go to bed at night and turn off the lights, the stars on your picture will glow in the dark. God made the stars and moon to shine at night and the sun to shine during the day. He made everything in our world just right so that we can live and grow.

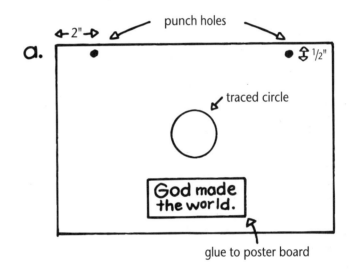

a.

b.

Blast-Off Rocket (25–30 MINUTES)

Materials
- ❏ Rocket Patterns
- ❏ star stickers
- ❏ hammer
- ❏ nail

For each child—
- ❏ one 10-oz. colored plastic cup
- ❏ one drinking straw

Standard Supplies
- ❏ photocopier
- ❏ copier paper or construction paper in various colors
- ❏ glue
- ❏ transparent tape
- ❏ scissors

Preparation
Photocopy Rocket Patterns onto several different colors of paper—at least one copy for each child. Use hammer and nail to pierce a hole in the center of the bottom of each cup, large enough for a drinking straw to fit through.

Instruct each child in the following procedures:

- Cut out all rocket pieces. Trade papers with someone to cut out different colors for different parts of your rocket.
- Glue a rocket fin on either side of rocket body strip at one end (sketch a).
- Tape drinking straw to bottom edge of strip between the two fins.
- Fold strip in half and glue rocket body closed over straw and fin edges.
- Fold remaining two rocket fins along dashed lines. Glue fin flaps to the center of each side of rocket body (sketch b).
- Glue one nose triangle to each side of top of rocket body, making edges even (sketch b).
- Decorate rocket with star stickers.
- Turn cup upside down. Insert straw through hole in cup. Rocket will rest near cup (sketch c).
- To launch your rocket, hold the end of the straw and push it up inside the cup as you count down from 10 to 1. Then say "Blast-off!" Twirl the straw as your rocket blasts off.

Lab Notes

You needed to follow my instructions to put your rocket together. You did a good job! What instructions did God give to Adam and Eve in the Garden of Eden? (They could eat from any tree except one.) **Did Adam and Eve follow God's instructions?** (No.) **Because Adam and Eve disobeyed God, sin entered our world. Sin separates people from God. But God had a plan to forgive all of our sins, so we can be in His family. He sent Jesus to take the punishment for the wrong things we do. If we believe in Jesus and tell God we're sorry, we can live with Him forever!**

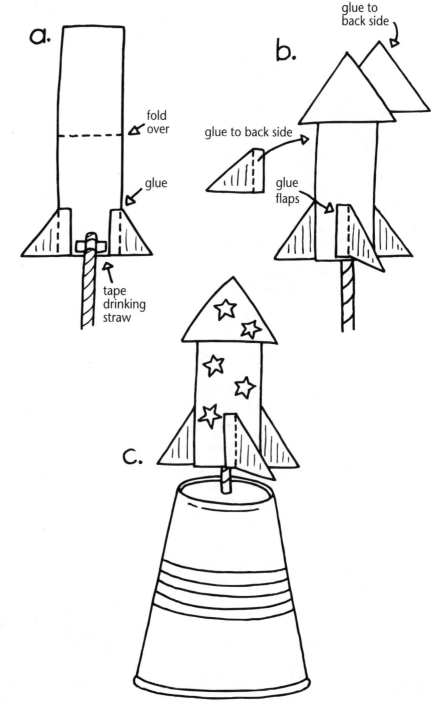

Rocket Patterns

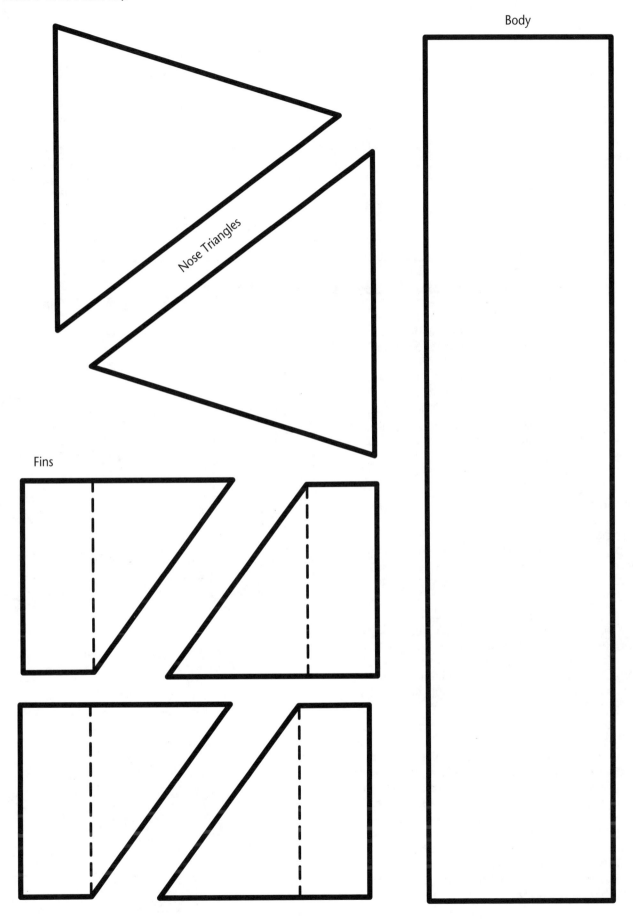

Body

Nose Triangles

Fins

Water Magnifier (25–30 MINUTES)

Materials

- ❏ flat white primer spray paint
- ❏ acrylic paints in various colors including green and blue
- ❏ plastic wrap
- ❏ disposable plastic plates

For each child—

- ❏ one small oatmeal container
- ❏ one 2½-inch (6.25-cm) rubber band
- ❏ viewing object such as a leaf, small rock, etc.

Standard Supplies

- ❏ scissors
- ❏ craft knife
- ❏ medium paintbrushes
- ❏ thin paintbrushes
- ❏ ruler
- ❏ water
- ❏ newspaper

Preparation

Use craft knife to cut three evenly spaced openings ¾ inch (1.9 cm) from the bottom of each container (sketch a). Openings should be 3 inches (7.5 cm) wide and 3½-inches (8.75 cm) tall. Lightly cut with the craft knife, making several passes to avoid crushing the cylinder. Lay newspaper on the ground in an outdoor area and spray oatmeal containers with white paint to cover completely. Cover work area in classroom with newspaper. Set out plastic plates and bottles of acrylic paints.

Instruct each child in the following procedures:

- Using medium-sized paintbrush, paint a nature scene to cover entire container on the outside. Squeeze a small amount of paint onto a portion of a plastic plate to use as a palette. Paint the container completely green for grass or all blue for sky. Or paint mountains, meadows, rivers, etc. to make a whole scene. Allow a few minutes to dry.

- Use a thin paintbrush to paint nature details like tall stems of grass, small flowers, butterflies, bugs, birds, clouds, etc. Leave the top 1 inch (2.5 cm) of container free from additional painting.

- Cut a piece of plastic wrap large enough to cover the top of the container. When paint on top portion of container is dry, loosely cover the container opening with the plastic, making a well, or "bowl" shape, so that plastic will hold water. To hold in place, place rubber band around plastic wrap about ½ inch (1.25 cm) from the top of container (sketch b). Trim excess plastic wrap if necessary.

- To use, set the magnifier in a lighted area. Pour a little water into the plastic wrap well. Set an object inside the magnifier and view through the water (sketch c). (*Note:* Teacher should provide a sample Water Magnifier for children to look through in class so that their own craft has ample time to dry before use.)

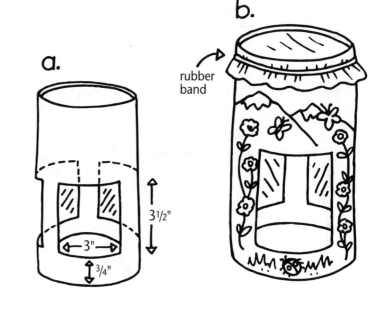

Lab Notes

The water in the plastic wrap makes a magnifying lens. When you look through it, what do you notice? (The object looks bigger. You can see it better.) **When Jesus came to earth, He helped us see God better. When we learn about Jesus, we learn what God is like. What do you know about how Jesus treated people? What are some kind things He did?** (Children respond.) **God is like that, too. He is kind and loving.**

Ring Around the Rocket (25–30 MINUTES)

Materials

- ¼-inch (.625-cm) dowels
- acrylic paints in various colors including metallic colors
- star garland wire
- electrical tape
- cotton string
- saw
- disposable plastic plates

For each child—

- three wooden spools in graduated sizes (available at craft stores)
- one mini shaker wooden peg (available at craft stores)
- one metallic chenille wire

Standard Supplies

- craft glue
- scissors
- sponge brushes
- medium paintbrushes
- measuring stick
- shallow containers
- newspaper

Preparation

Use saw to cut dowels into 12-inch (30-cm) lengths—one for each child. Cut string into 24-inch (60-cm) lengths—one for each child. Cut garland wire into 12-inch (30-cm) lengths—one for each child. Pour glue into shallow containers. Squeeze several small puddles of different colored paints onto plastic plates. Cover work area with newspaper.

Instruct each child in the following procedures:

- Use sponge brush to apply glue to half of dowel.
- Slide the three spools onto glued part of dowel, largest to smallest, to make rocket. The last spool should extend about ¼ inch (.625 cm) past the end of dowel. Brush some glue onto the end of peg and insert into the spool hole (sketch a).
- Paint the wooden spools and peg to look like a rocket. You may want to paint each part a separate color. Allow paint to dry.
- Wrap garland wire around chenille wire (sketch b).
- Bend both wires into a circle and twist ends together to make a ring (sketch c).
- Tie one end of string to star ring. Then tie other end around dowel below the bottom spool.
- Wrap a piece of tape around the dowel and over the tied string to secure string (sketch d).
- When paint is dry, hold dowel upright, swing the ring into the air and try to catch it on the rocket.

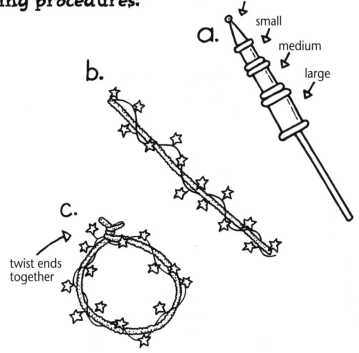

Lab Notes

People who study the universe are called astronomers. Have you ever looked through a telescope at night? What did you see? Astronomers have learned a lot about planets far, far away. Rockets have even been sent to our moon and to other planets. People have created some amazing things that have helped us learn about the universe. But God created the whole universe! And He created people with minds that can ask questions and learn about God's world.

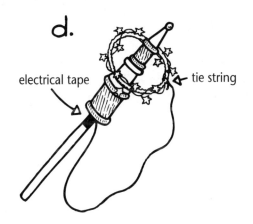

Creation Sphere (TWO-DAY CRAFT/15–20 MINUTES EACH DAY)

Materials
- ❏ white foamboard (available at craft stores)
- ❏ black poster paint
- ❏ dish soap
- ❏ star garland wire
- ❏ string
- ❏ globe or large picture of earth from space

For each child—
- ❏ one toothpick

Standard Supplies
- ❏ crayons in various colors including blue and green
- ❏ pencil
- ❏ scissors
- ❏ craft knife
- ❏ paintbrushes
- ❏ shallow containers
- ❏ newspaper
- ❏ measuring stick

Day One Preparation

Draw a 12-inch (30-cm) diameter circle on foamboard and use craft knife to cut out—one for each child. Draw a 10-inch (25-cm) circle inside of each foamboard circle and use craft knife to cut out smaller circle—one for each child (sketch a). Pour black paint into shallow containers and add a drop of dish soap to each container. Cover work area with newspaper. Display globe or picture of earth.

Instruct each child in the following procedures:

- Color both sides of ring cutout with a blue crayon.
- Use several different colors of crayons to color one side of circle. Press hard to make a thick layer of crayon, covering circle completely.
- Color the other side of circle with blue and green crayons to look like the earth (sketch b).
- Paint a layer of black paint over heavily crayoned side of circle. Set aside to dry.

Day Two Preparation

Cut string into 12-inch (30-cm) lengths—one for each child. Cut garland wire into 2-foot (.6-m) lengths—two for each child.

Instruct each child in the following procedures:

- As teacher talks about God creating the earth, use a toothpick to scratch pictures into the painted surface to make a creation scene. (*Note:* Ideas for scene and suggested teacher conversation below.)
- With teacher's help, place garland around outer edge of half of ring and insert ends into foam to secure in place (sketch c). Place other garland length around other half of ring in a similar manner.
- Place circle inside ring and insert toothpick through the top of ring and into the top of circle (sketch d). Tie one end of string around top of ring. Tie loop in the other end of string for hanging.

Lab Notes

Before God created the world, there was only darkness—just like your circle is completely black. First God created the heavens and the earth. Your circle is the earth and the ring is the heavens. On the second day God created sky and water. What kind of water can you draw on the black side of your circle? (Ocean. Lakes. Rivers.) **On the third day God created the dry land and plants. What kind of land can you draw?** (Flat land. Hills. Valleys. Mountains.) **What kind of plants can you draw?** (Grass. Flowers. Trees.) **On the fourth day God created the sun, the moon and the stars. Draw a sun if you want to make a picture of the daytime, or a moon and stars if you want to draw night. On the fifth day God created birds and fish. What kind of birds can you draw?** (Ducks. Pigeons. Seagulls. Eagles.) **What kind of fish can you draw?** (Goldfish. Trout. Sharks. Whales.) **On the sixth day God created animals and man. What kind of animals can you draw?** (Allow volunteers to answer.) **What person or people will you make in your picture?**

    Our Bible says that on the seventh day God rested, and now you can take a rest because your creation is complete. God looked at everything He created and said, "It is good!" When I look at the pictures you just created, I can say "It is good!" too.

a.

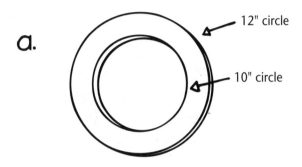

12" circle

10" circle

b.

back side of circle

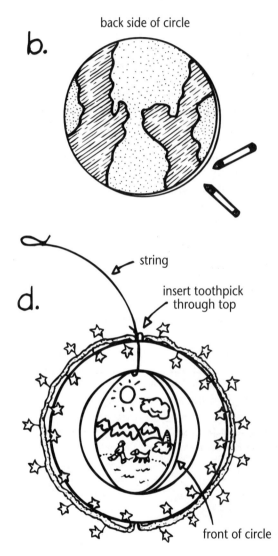

string

insert toothpick
through top

c.

insert wire ends into foam

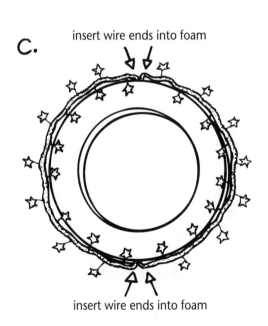

insert wire ends into foam

d.

front of circle

RovingRobot (ONE- OR TWO-DAY CRAFT/40–45 MINUTES TOTAL TIME)

Materials

- ❑ Fun Foam in a variety of colors (available at craft stores)
- ❑ brightly colored bendable drinking straws
- ❑ fine-tip fabric paints
- ❑ transparent colored pony beads
- ❑ small acrylic jewels and/or sequins in a variety of sizes and shapes
- ❑ aluminum foil
- ❑ small plastic lids and caps
- ❑ thin metallic gift ribbon
- ❑ craft sticks

For each child—
- ❑ one large empty thread spool
- ❑ one 16- to 18-oz. colored plastic cup
- ❑ one small colored plastic plate
- ❑ one small bathroom-sized paper cup
- ❑ two metallic chenille wires, plus some extras

Standard Supplies

- ❑ pens
- ❑ extra thick craft glue
- ❑ scissors
- ❑ hole punch
- ❑ measuring stick

Day One Preparation

Set plastic cup upside down in the center of a plastic plate and trace around cup. Cut out circle ½ inch (1.25 cm) smaller than traced line. Repeat with remaining plates. Punch two holes in the curved part of plate rims, directly opposite each other (sketch a). Cut the bendable end of straws into 4-inch (10-cm) lengths—two for each child. Reserve the straight part of straws for decorating and for Day Two. Cut some of the chenille wires in half—two halves for each child. Cut Fun Foam into 5-inch (12.5-cm) squares.

Instruct each child in the following procedures:

- Lay plate down with the bottom facing up. Use craft stick to spread glue on the rim of large cup and then glue cup onto plate, covering the cutout circle. This is the robot's body.
- Cut a square of Fun Foam into any shape a little smaller than the size of the square. Punch two holes in the edge of Fun Foam shape, spacing the holes far apart and directly opposite each other (sketch b).
- To make arms, thread a 6-inch (15-cm) chenille wire through a 4-inch (10-cm) piece of drinking straw and allow the wire to stick out of each end.
- Thread one end of wire through hole in Fun Foam, double wire back and insert into straw end. Thread a bead on opposite end of wire for hand. Glue or bend wire around bead to secure (sketch b). Repeat for each arm.
- Glue the foam piece to the top of cup, making sure the arms line up with holes in the plate rim (sketch c).
- Cover the small paper cup with one or two pieces of foil to make robot's head.
- For ears, eyes and mouth, glue on beads, sequins, small pieces of chenille wire, small Fun Foam shapes or pony beads (sketch d).
- Glue items to the top of robot head to decorate: small lids, pieces of Fun Foam, chenille wires and beads.
- Spread glue on the rim of the robot head and glue on top of the Fun Foam, centering the head between the arms.

Day Two Preparation

Cut metallic gift ribbon into 1-yard (.9-m) lengths— one for each child.

Instruct each child in the following procedures:

- Thread one long chenille wire through a straight 4-inch (10-cm) piece of drinking straw. Thread the spool onto the straw.
- Lay your robot on its back with the underside of plate facing you (sketch e). Insert the wire ends through the two holes in the rim of plate. Bend the wire ends around the plate rim and run them through the holes again. Twist wires to secure.
- With hole punch, punch a hole in the plate rim at the center front of robot. Tie ribbon through the hole for toy pull.
- Set the robot upright. Decorate your robot body. Cut Fun Foam into small shapes and glue on for instrument panels and a computer screen. Glue on acrylic jewels, sequins and beads for buttons (sketch f).
- Carefully use fabric paint to draw lines, dots or geometric designs on plate base or cup body. Allow to dry several hours.
- Pull the ribbon to make your robot move at your command!

Simplification Idea

Use brightly colored card stock in place of Fun Foam.

Lab Notes

Some robots do work that is dangerous for humans to do. Some robots work in factories and do tasks that are tiring for people. Robots can help us. But humans are even better at helping each other! We can be kind to people. We can cheer people up. We can show God's love to people who don't know about Jesus. What could you do to show love or help someone you know?

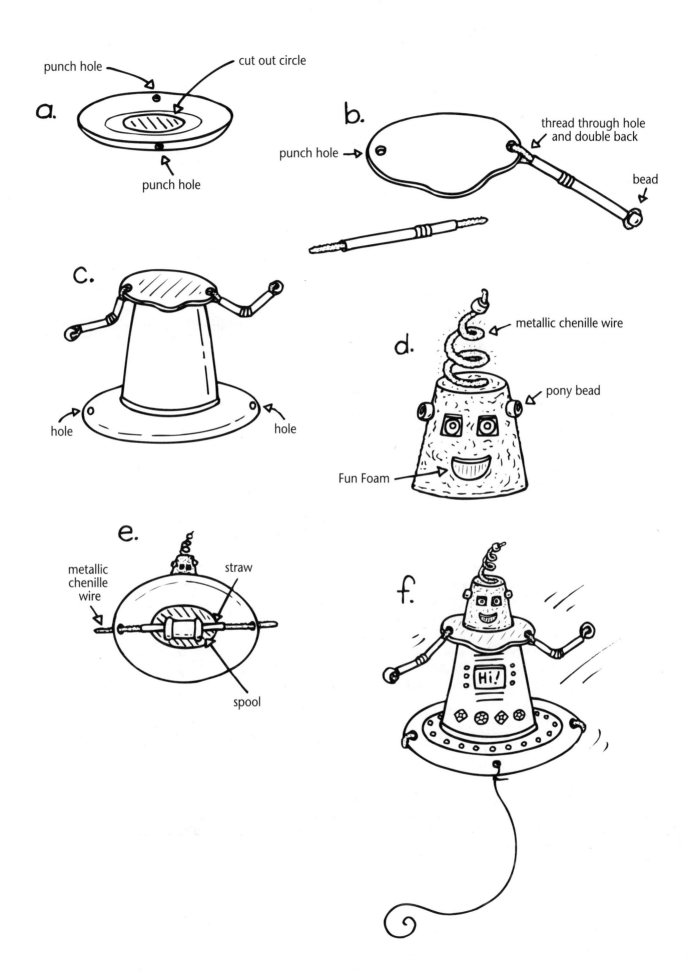

a. punch hole   cut out circle   punch hole

b. punch hole   thread through hole and double back   bead

c. hole   hole

d. metallic chenille wire   pony bead   Fun Foam

e. metallic chenille wire   straw   spool

f. Hi!

Creation Mobile (ONE- OR TWO-DAY CRAFT/40–45 MINUTES TOTAL TIME)

Materials

- ❏ Creation Mobile Patterns (p.50)
- ❏ crochet thread
- ❏ drinking straws
- ❏ assorted small nature stickers
- ❏ medium- to large-sized plastic and acrylic beads
- ❏ Fun Foam in various colors (available at craft stores)
- ❏ hand or power drill
- ❏ 1/16-inch (.156-cm) drill bit
- ❏ permanent felt pens

For each child—
- ❏ one 2-liter plastic soda bottle with cap
- ❏ three short 8-oz. clear plastic cups

Standard Supplies

- ❏ lightweight cardboard
- ❏ pens
- ❏ transparent tape
- ❏ scissors
- ❏ hole punch
- ❏ measuring stick

Preparation

Cut drinking straws into the following lengths: 4 inches (10 cm)—three for each child; 2 inches (5 cm)—four for each child. Cut crochet thread into the following lengths: 30 inches (75 cm)—one for each child; 25 inches (62.5 cm)—three for each child. Use drill to make a hole in the center of the bottle caps and the center bottom of each plastic cup. For each bottle: Place cap on bottle. Cut bottle 4 inches (10 cm) down from top. Discard bottom portion (sketch a). Punch three evenly spaced holes along the bottom edge of bottle. Trace Creation Mobile Patterns onto lightweight cardboard, at least two copies of each shape. Cut out.

Instruct each child in the following procedures:

- Place a few stickers on the bottle and on each of the cups.
- With pen, trace four different Creation Patterns onto various colors of Fun Foam. Cut out.
- Use a hole punch to make a hole near the top edge of each shape (sketch b).
- Thread the 30-inch (75-cm) length of crochet thread through the hole in one Fun Foam shape.
- Make the ends of the thread even. With teacher's help, wrap tape around thread ends to make a "needle" (sketch c).
- String 10 to 14 beads on the doubled thread. Add a 2-inch (5-cm) straw piece and then thread needle through the underside of the bottle cap and out the top (sketch d).
- String one more bead onto needle and then thread needle through the bead again to secure bead to bottle top (sketch e). Remove tape on thread ends and tie ends together in a knot.
- Insert a 25-inch (62.5-cm) length of crochet thread through the hole in another Fun Foam shape, pull the ends even and wrap with tape to make needle.
- String two beads, a 4-inch (10-cm) straw piece and two more beads.
- Entering from the inside of one plastic cup, thread needle through the hole in cup bottom. Then string a bead, a 2-inch (5-cm) straw piece and one more bead. Remove tape and tie ends to a punched hole in bottle, with the bead close to bottle edge (sketch f). Trim ends.
- Repeat instructions to attach the two remaining cups (sketch g).

Simplification Idea

Purchase precut Fun Foam nature shapes (available at craft supply stores). Instead of using plastic cups, straws and beads, attach shapes directly onto bottle.

Lab Notes

It's amazing how many different kinds of creatures and creations God has made. How many sea creatures can you name? birds? insects? mammals? reptiles? What about people? In what way are all people the same? In what way are we different? I'm glad God created so many different people and things. He made our world an interesting place to live!

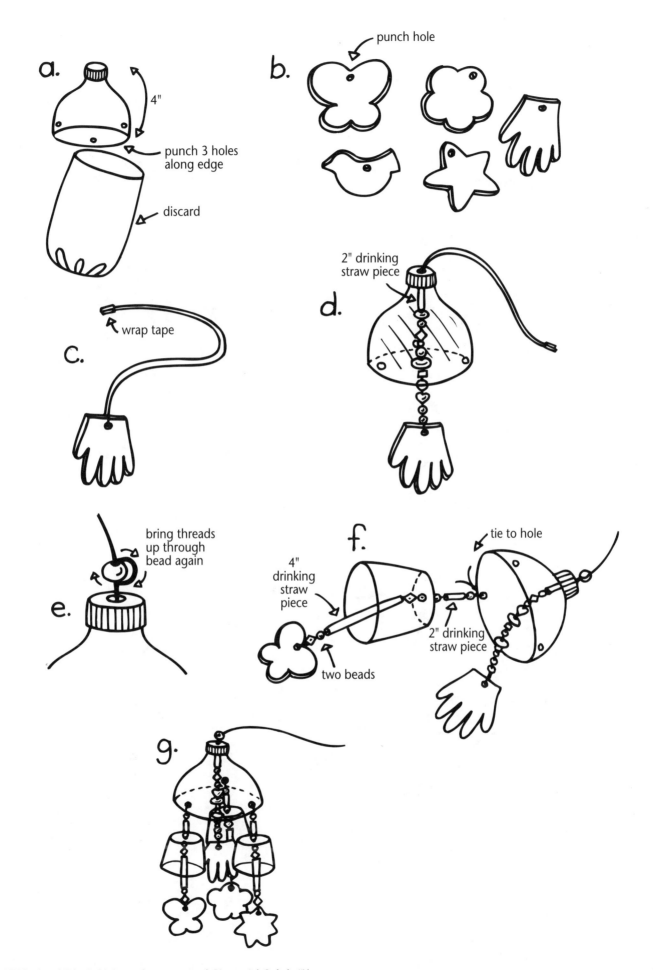

a.
4"
punch 3 holes along edge
discard

b.
punch hole

c.
wrap tape

d.
2" drinking straw piece

e.
bring threads up through bead again

f.
4" drinking straw piece
two beads
2" drinking straw piece
tie to hole

g.

Creation Mobile Patterns

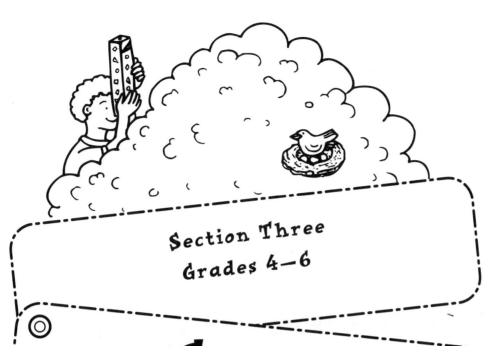

Section Three
Grades 4—6

Crafts for
Older Elementary

Trying to plan craft projects for older children has driven many teachers prematurely gray. The challenge is that while these children have well-developed skills to complete projects, they also have well-developed preferences about what they want to do. Thus a project that challenges their abilities may be scorned because it is somehow not appealing to these young sophisticates. Then the next project will seem too juvenile to the adult but will click with the kids!

We think you'll find projects in this section to satisfy the varied tastes of older elementary children. But a sense of humor and these tips will surely help: Filter a craft idea through a panel of experts—two or three fifth graders. If they like it, chances are the rest of the group will. Also, the better you get to know your students, the better your batting average will be.

Galaxy Glitter Tube (10–15 MINUTES)

Materials

- ❏ ¾-inch (1.9-cm) clear vinyl tubing (available at home-improvement stores)
- ❏ star and moon plastic confetti
- ❏ glitter
- ❏ blue food coloring
- ❏ pitcher
- ❏ several funnels
- ❏ heavy-duty scissors

For each child—
- ❏ two corks to fit the ends of tubing

Standard Supplies

- ❏ measuring stick
- ❏ disposable cups
- ❏ water
- ❏ low-temperature glue gun and glue sticks

Preparation

With heavy-duty scissors, cut tubing into 18-inch (45-cm) lengths—one for each child. Plug in glue gun out of reach of children. Fill pitcher with water.

Instruct each child in the following procedures:

- With teacher's help, apply glue from glue gun around the circumference of one cork. Quickly push cork into one end of tube to seal the end of tube (sketch a). Allow glue to cool a minute or two.

- Place two or three pinches of confetti into tube. Add a pinch or two of glitter.

- Pour water into a cup. Add a few drops of blue food coloring to cup. Use a funnel to pour water from the cup *slowly* into the tube (tube will fill quickly). Fill tube to within 1½ inches (3.75 cm) from the top (sketch b).

- Hold tube upright. Have teacher squeeze glue from glue gun around the second cork. Push cork into end of tube. Allow glue to cool a minute or two to make sure glue seals tube end.

- Tip the tube back and forth to mix the food coloring with the water (sketch c). Watch the stars glitter in space!

Lab Notes

Look for the bubble in your tube. Your Galaxy Glitter Tube works the same as a carpenter's level. Someone long ago discovered that a bubble would stay in the center of a tube of water if the tube was laid on a level surface. Straighten out your tube and lay it on the table. Is the table level? Simple inventions like the level are important to our lives every day. What are some other inventions that we use every day?

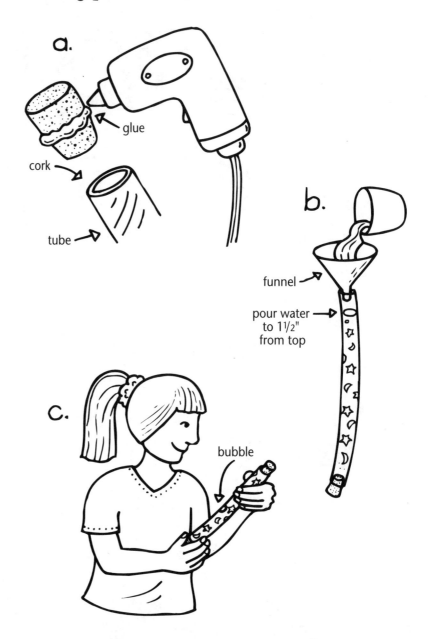

a.

glue

cork

tube

b.

funnel

pour water to 1½" from top

c.

bubble

"Metal Head" Robot (20–25 MINUTES)

Materials

- ❑ jump rings
- ❑ sequin bangles
- ❑ pony beads
- ❑ assorted plastic lids and caps from food/toiletry containers
- ❑ 5-inch (12.5-cm) clear or colored plastic bowls
- ❑ short clear or colored plastic cups
- ❑ shredded mylar gift filler
- ❑ high-tack adhesive (such as E-6000 or Goop)
- ❑ craft sticks and toothpicks
- ❑ various small hardware items (assorted mirror fasteners, furniture leg tips, self-stick bumpers, nylon and metal washers, screw covers, rubber rings, assorted nuts and wing nuts, sawtooth picture hangers, etc.)

For each child—
- ❑ one new, empty gallon- or quart-sized paint can with lid and no label (available at paint or home-improvement stores)

Standard Supplies

- ❑ scrap paper
- ❑ hole punch
- ❑ shallow containers

Preparation

Set out supplies, placing hardware items in separate shallow containers.

Instruct each child in the following procedures:

- Squeeze some adhesive onto scrap paper. Use craft stick or toothpick to apply adhesive to items.
- Glue two items on can to make robot eyes. Make sure they are centered from left to right between sides of handle (if using a gallon can).
- Embellish eyes with other items to make pupils and eyebrows (see sketch).
- Glue on items to make nose and mouth, layering items if desired.
- At the pail's "temples," glue a small arrangement of nuts, washers, etc. or shredded mylar to make hair.
- Make earrings for a girl robot: Insert jump rings in sequin holes and attach to sides of pail around handle or glue with adhesive. Make longer earrings by punching a hole in the bottom of first sequin and attaching another sequin with a jump ring.
- For robot's ears, glue wing nuts on sides of pail.
- Make hats or caps for a boy or girl robot. Place a small amount of shredded mylar in a clear plastic bowl or cup. Glue rim-down to the center of the paint can lid. Glue and stack colorful plastic lids on top of paint can lid and cover with a clear bowl or cup. Colored plastic cups or bowls could also be used alone as hats and embellished with small items as desired.
- Allow adhesive to dry overnight.
- Use your robot to store toys, candy or any other items!

Lab Notes

A real robot is a combination of a mechanical machine and a computer. Like a machine, it has moving parts. Like a computer, it can be programmed to do certain tasks. Today, some robots even have sensors that help them see, hear and feel. Robots are used to work on assembly lines in factories or to do tasks that are dangerous for people to do, like handling toxic materials. Even though robots can do many things, what can people do that a robot can never do? (Love someone, cry, sleep, play soccer, pray, etc.) **People are God's ultimate creation. He even made us capable of creating amazing things—such as robots!**

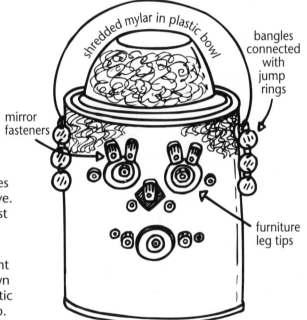

shredded mylar in plastic bowl

bangles connected with jump rings

mirror fasteners

furniture leg tips

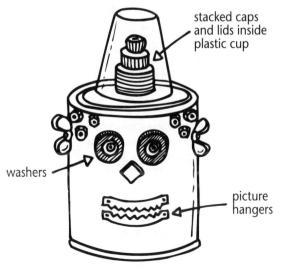

stacked caps and lids inside plastic cup

washers

picture hangers

Frenetic-Kinetic Machine (20–25 MINUTES)

Materials

- ❏ metallic confetti or glitter
- ❏ paint pens or permanent felt pens in various colors
- ❏ string
- ❏ hand or power drill
- ❏ ¼-inch (.625-cm) drill bit

For each child—

- ❏ 28-oz. clear plastic peanut butter jar and lid with label removed
- ❏ three large metal nuts
- ❏ one 3x1/8-inch (7.5x.312-cm) rubber band
- ❏ two toothpicks

Standard Supplies

- ❏ scissors
- ❏ ruler

Preparation

Use drill and bit to make a hole in the center of each lid and bottom of each jar. Cut string into 6-inch (15-cm) lengths.

Instruct each child in the following procedures:

- Secure nuts together by threading string piece through the center of the three nuts and tie in a knot. Lay the rubber band on top of knot. Tie and knot string around rubber band (sketch a).
- Place the nuts and rubber band inside the jar. Thread one end of rubber band through the hole in the bottom of jar.
- Insert a toothpick through rubber band loop to hold it in place (sketch b). Break ends of toothpick off to make it about 1 inch (2.5 cm) long.
- Pull the other end of rubber band out of the jar. Ask a partner to hold the jar lid while you push the rubber band through the hole in the lid. Insert toothpick to hold in place and break off ends as in previous step (sketch c).
- Pull jar lid away from opening and place some confetti and/or glitter inside jar.
- Screw lid on jar.
- Decorate jar with paint pens or felt pens as desired (sketch d). Allow paint to dry.
- Slowly roll your jar across a flat, smooth surface such as a table or linoleum floor. It will roll back to you!

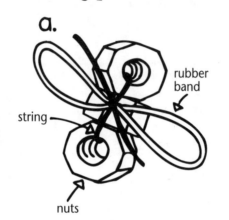

a.

rubber band

string

nuts

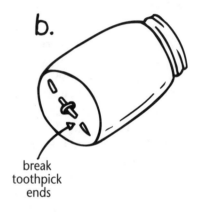

b.

break toothpick ends

c. toothpick

d. decorate with pens

confetti

Lab Notes

Your rolling jar contains something called kinetic energy. Motion is a form of kinetic energy. As the jar rolls, the rubber band twists and stores up that energy. When the jar stops, the rubber band unwinds and releases the stored-up energy, making the jar roll backwards.

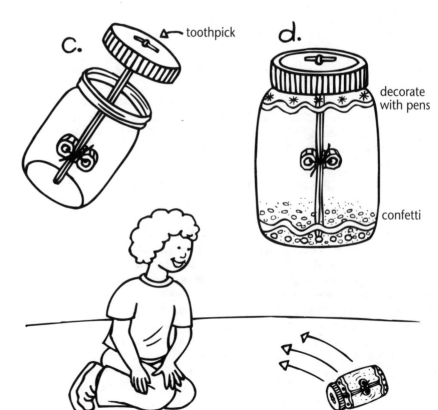

You-Name-It Concoction (20–25 MINUTES)

Materials

❏ liquid starch
❏ primer spray paint
❏ spray paint in bright colors
❏ food coloring
❏ several ¼- or ⅓-cup measuring cups
❏ permanent felt pens or paint pens in several colors

For each child—

❏ one margarine, cottage cheese or yogurt container with resealable lid
❏ one large disposable plastic cup
❏ one heavy-duty plastic spoon

Standard Supplies

❏ white glue
❏ pencils
❏ newspaper

Preparation

Spread newspaper in an open area and spray a coat of primer on containers and lids. Allow to dry and then spray with one or two coats of spray paint, allowing to dry between coats.

Instruct each child in the following procedures:

- Fill a measuring cup with white glue. Pour into large plastic cup.
- Fill same-sized measuring cup with liquid starch. Pour into plastic cup.
- Add a few drops of food coloring to plastic cup.
- Use spoon to mix glue, starch and food coloring together until "goopy." Set aside mixture (sketch a).
- Decide what your concoction will be named: Dr. Wonder's Zloop, Professor (Your Name)'s Ooze, Glorious Gloop, Blue Goo, etc.
- Decorate the spray-painted container and lid to look like the packaging for your invention. With a pencil, first write the name of your concoction on the container. Draw designs and/or letter words to describe your new product. Then trace over penciled name and designs with felt pens or paint pens (sketch b).
- Pour your mixture from the plastic cup into the decorated container. Place lid securely on top.
- Have fun playing with the gooey, slimy, oozy stuff that *you* created! Or give it to a friend! (*Note:* Your concoction may stick to carpet or fabric. Keep mixture covered when not it use. If mixture sits a long time, it may separate. If that happens, pour off liquid; mixture will then resemble Silly Putty!)

Lab Notes

The mixture you made today is similar to products sold in toy stores. You found out that it is really very easy to make. Someone, somehow, discovered that glue and liquid starch mixed together would be a fun thing to play with. How do you think people make these discoveries? (By trying, failing and trying again with something different. By accident, etc.) **When God made the world, He didn't have to experiment. God designed our world with a purpose in mind— to be a home for people who would love Him and whom He could love in return.**

a.

b.

Creation Kid (20–25 MINUTES)

Instruct each child in the following procedures:

- Choose a large bead for the head of your Creation Kid. Thread all eight wire strands through large bead allowing approximately 2 inches (5 cm) of wire to extend from the top of bead for "hair."

- Using a bamboo skewer, coil each "hair" wire, if desired. You may also add small beads to wires. Bend wire ends to secure beads on wire (sketch a).

- Thread a smaller bead below the head for the neck or collar.

- Separate one strand for the right arm and one strand for the left arm. Thread several beads onto arms and then add one small bead for each hand. Bend the strands over the small bead and thread back through the arm beads, returning to the wire torso (sketch b).

- Hold all the unbeaded wires together and thread on two or three large beads for the torso.

- Divide strands into two separate bundles for the legs (sketch c). Thread eight to ten beads on each leg, leaving about 2 inches (5 cm) of wire unbeaded.

- Use pliers to bend wire ends to form feet and to keep beads in place (sketch d). Twist ends tightly.

- Attach your Creation Kid to the key ring by coiling one of the wire hairs around key ring.

Lab Notes

You can bend your Creation Kid into many different positions. Can you make it leap? sit? dance? pray? Your Creation Kid can remind you that God created you with many different abilities. People are God's most incredible creation. What are some things people can do that the rest of God's creations can't do?

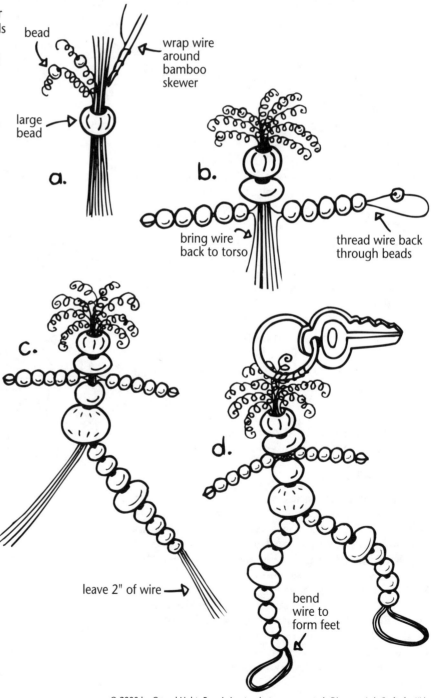

bead

wrap wire around bamboo skewer

large bead

a.

b.

bring wire back to torso

thread wire back through beads

c.

d.

leave 2" of wire →

bend wire to form feet

The Incredible Self-Watering Seed Starter (25–30 MINUTES)

Materials

- ❏ fabric paints in various colors
- ❏ potting soil
- ❏ easy-to-grow seeds (sunflower, bean, nasturtium, etc.)
- ❏ large plastic tub or container
- ❏ pitchers of water
- ❏ permanent felt pen

For each child—
- ❏ one 1- or 2-liter clear plastic soda bottle with label removed

Standard Supplies

- ❏ craft knife
- ❏ sharp scissors
- ❏ ruler
- ❏ disposable cups
- ❏ paper towels

Preparation

Draw a line evenly around each bottle with permanent felt pen, about 5 inches (12.5 cm) from the top. Use craft knife to make a 1-inch (2.5-cm) slit along line. Pour potting soil into large tub or container.

Instruct each child in the following procedures:

- Use scissors to cut bottle in two. Begin at slit and cut along pen line (sketch a).
- Use fabric paint to decorate the bottom portion of bottle. Draw a nature design of plants, bugs and butterflies or other creations that God has made. Leave the top 5 inches (12.5 cm) undecorated (sketch b).
- Fill one-third of bottle with water (sketch c). Set in a place away from work area.
- Cut a paper towel in half. Tightly roll one half into a rope.
- Turn top portion of bottle upside down, like a funnel, and insert one end of rolled paper towel into the mouth of the bottle (sketch d).
- Stuff other half of paper towel into the mouth of the funnel around the paper towel rope to block the opening and hold rope in place.
- Use a cup to fill the funnel with soil.
- With fingers, push a few seeds into the soil next to the funnel sides, so you can see the seeds through the plastic (sketch e).
- Carefully set the funnel in the top of painted bottle bottom, being careful not to touch wet paint. The paper towel rope should extend into the water in the bottle.
- Pour a little water into the soil to dampen seeds.
- Allow paint on bottle to dry before taking home.

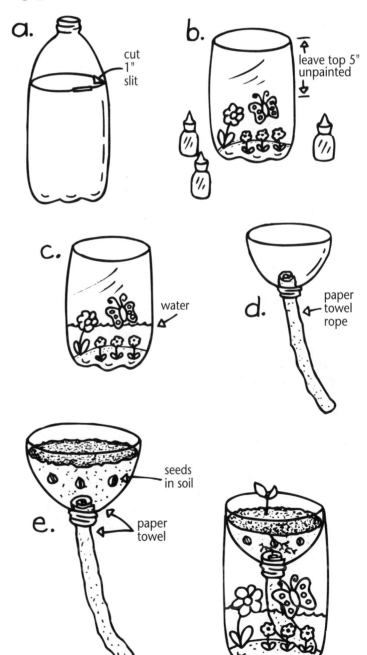

Lab Notes

You invented a way of watering your seeds automatically. How do you think your seeds receive water? (The paper towel rope hangs in the water below. The water is absorbed through the paper towel and travels up to the soil, which absorbs the water.) **If you keep enough water in the bottom of your planter so that the paper towel is always wet, you can go a week or more without watering your seeds or plants. As you watch your seeds sprout, have fun observing how God has created plants to grow!**

Up Periscope! (25–30 MINUTES)

Materials
- ❑ Periscope Pattern
- ❑ corrugated cardboard
- ❑ primer or flat black spray paint
- ❑ silver metallic spray paint
- ❑ cellophane in various colors
- ❑ high-tack adhesive (such as E-6000 or Goop)

For each child—
- ❑ two 1½-inch (3.75-cm) square mirrors (available at craft supply stores)
- ❑ one 18-inch (45-cm) aluminum foil or plastic wrap box

Standard Supplies
- ❑ pen
- ❑ hot glue gun and glue sticks
- ❑ glue sticks
- ❑ masking tape
- ❑ scissors
- ❑ craft knife
- ❑ rulers
- ❑ newspaper

Preparation
Cut cardboard into 1 3/4x5½-inch (4.4x13.75-cm) strips—two for each child. Use pen to mark Periscope Pattern folding lines on each cardboard strip. Prepare each foil box as follows: Place a strip of masking tape over serrated metal edge. Cut off the inner flap on the right side of box. Then cut a 2-inch (5-cm) square at the right end of lid, leaving outer flap intact (sketch a). Using hot glue gun, glue the outer flap to the box to permanently close lid. Turn box over. Use craft knife to cut a 2-inch (5-cm) square out of the left end of box bottom (sketch b). Cover outdoor area with newspaper and paint boxes with primer or black spray paint to cover package design. Then spray with silver paint to cover all sides.

Instruct each child in the following procedures:

- Cover the backside of each mirror with masking tape to prevent the pieces from scattering if mirrors get dropped and broken. Trim off any excess tape.
- Place ruler along fold line on one cardboard strip and then fold up against the ruler edge to make crease (sketch c). Repeat to crease the other line. Fold cardboard strip into a triangular wedge and tape ends together (sketch d).
- Repeat procedure to form the other cardboard strip into a wedge.
- Squeeze adhesive onto the back of each mirror and position on the large face (opposite the right angle) of each cardboard wedge (sketch e).
- To decorate periscope box, cut colored cellophane into small geometric shapes. Rub glue stick onto cellophane pieces and glue pieces to box randomly.
- Squeeze adhesive onto the two remaining surfaces of each cardboard wedge. Set wedges into the 2-inch (5-cm) openings of periscope box, gluing to the ends and sides of box (sketch f).
- Use your periscope to see around a wall or over a fence.

Lab Notes
Periscopes were invented for submarines. Periscopes allowed the people aboard to see above the water when they were submerged. How could you use your periscope? (To see around corners or over fences or walls.) **Periscopes work because the mirror next to your eye is reflecting the object in the other mirror, which in turn is reflecting the real object. The mirrors in your periscope are a good example of what Jesus did for us. We see more of what God is like because Jesus mirrored God's image to us. When we learn about Jesus and how He lived, we can see God and know how much He loves us.**

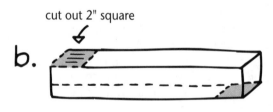

a.

glue flap with hot glue

cut 2" square

cut off flap

cut serrated edge with tape

foil

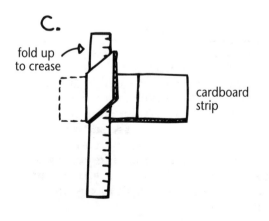

b.

cut out 2" square

c.

fold up to crease

cardboard strip

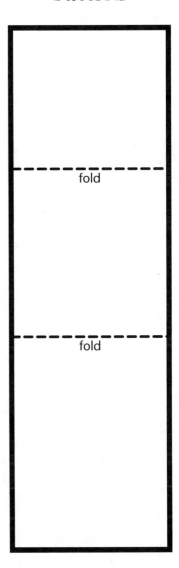

Periscope Pattern

fold

fold

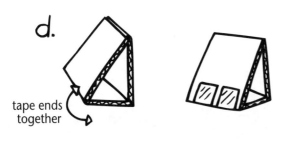

d.

tape ends together

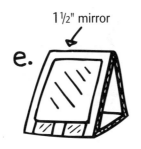

1½" mirror

e.

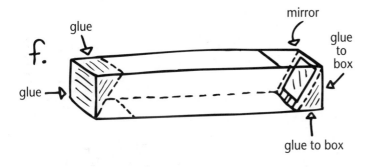

f.

glue

mirror

glue to box

glue

glue to box

Space-Rock Secret Safe (25–30 MINUTES)

Materials

❏ sheets of Fun Foam in various colors (available at craft stores)
❏ aquarium pebbles in several colors
❏ paint pens or permanent felt pens
❏ facial tissues

For each child—
❏ one small plastic peanut butter jar and lid, label removed
❏ one cardboard tube

Standard Supplies

❏ pencils
❏ craft glue
❏ scissors

Preparation

Cut tubes into lengths that equal the depths of jars when tubes are placed inside.

Instruct each child in the following procedures:

- Place end of tube on a piece of Fun Foam and trace around it, adding about ¼ inch (.625 cm) to its circumference. Cut out foam circle.
- Squeeze glue around edge of one end of tube. Place foam circle on glued end of tube (sketch a). Set aside to dry.
- Trace around the peanut butter jar lid on a piece of Fun Foam. Cut out circle.
- Set foam circle on top of jar lid. Trim if needed to fit on top of lid. Glue foam circle to top of lid (sketch b).
- Cut out small foam shapes in contrasting colors and glue to lid to decorate.
- Lay jar on its side and fill with a layer of pebbles about ½ inch (1.25 cm) deep (sketch c). Center the tube inside the jar, making sure the foam end is resting against the bottom of the jar.
- Carefully set jar upright, holding the tube in place. Allow the pebbles to fill in around the tube to keep the tube upright (sketch d).
- Gently stuff tissues inside the tube to keep pebbles from falling in while filling jar.
- Carefully fill jar to the top with pebbles. You may want to layer pebbles of different colors.
- Remove tissues from tube. Screw lid onto jar.
- Use paint pens or felt pens to write "My Space Rock Collection" on the jar (sketch e). You may want to label specific colored rocks as if from Mars, Neptune, the Moon, etc.
- You may fill the tube with small treasures. The tube should be completely concealed. No one will know your space rock collection is really your secret safe!

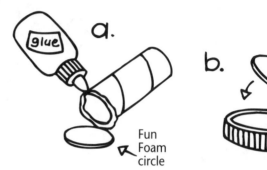

Fun Foam circle

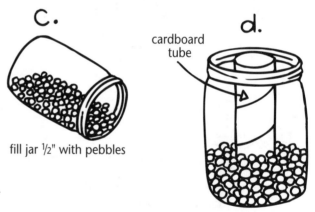

fill jar ½" with pebbles

cardboard tube

Lab Notes

What could you keep in your Space-Rock Secret Safe? Probably no one will believe your "rock collection" is from outer space. But astronauts really have brought back rocks from the moon. The rocks are displayed in many different museums around the country. Some planets would be difficult to get rocks from. Why is that? (Some planets are mostly gas. Many have atmospheres that make it difficult to land. Many planets are too far away.) **God made more stars and planets than scientists can count or see. Even though astronomers have learned many things about outer space, most of God's endless universe is still a mystery.**

My Space Rock Collection

Futuristic Frame (25–30 MINUTES)

Materials

- ❏ Strato-core or foamboard (available at craft stores)
- ❏ magnet strips
- ❏ plastic canvas in various bright colors
- ❏ flexible plastic drinking straws in various bright colors
- ❏ pony beads in various colors
- ❏ high-tack adhesive (such as E-6000 or Goop)
- ❏ toothpicks and craft sticks

Optional—
- ❏ camera and film

Standard Supplies

- ❏ scrap paper
- ❏ craft knife
- ❏ scissors
- ❏ ruler

Preparation

Use craft knife to cut Strato-core or foamboard into 5x8-inch (12.5x20-cm) rectangles and 1x5-inch (2.5x 12.5-cm) strips—one rectangle and two strips for each child. Cut magnet strips into 4-inch (10-cm) lengths—two for each child. Cut plastic canvas into rectangles about 2x3 inches (5x7.5 cm). (*Optional:* One or two days before children make project, take a vertical photo of each child and develop film into 4x6-inch [10x15-cm] prints.)

Instruct each child in the following procedures:

- Squeeze a small amount of adhesive onto scrap paper. Use a toothpick or craft stick to apply adhesive.
- Position back of board rectangle vertically and use adhesive to glue one magnet strip about 1 inch (2.5 cm) from top and the other strip the same distance from the bottom (sketch a).
- Glue the two board strips to the front of rectangle at the top and bottom, edges even with board (sketch b).
- Choose several different colors of plastic canvas pieces to decorate frame. Cut some pieces into various smaller geometric shapes. Then glue pieces onto board strips, extending pieces beyond the edges of strips. First glue the larger pieces in a single layer and then overlap with smaller pieces (sketch c).
- Cut drinking straws into various-sized pieces. Cut ends at an angle. Bend the flexible portion of straw pieces and glue on top of plastic canvas pieces (sketch d).
- Glue on beads and any other bits of plastic canvas scraps and straws as desired (sketch e). Allow glue to dry.
- You can put your frame on your refrigerator at home and slide a 4x6-inch (10x15-cm) photograph in place. The plastic canvas pieces that overlap the inner edge of strips will keep the photo in place.

Enrichment Idea

If using plastic Strato-core board, frames may also be used as a write-on message board. Provide each child ith a dry-erase marker.

Lab Notes

What do you think you will be doing in the future? Often we think of the future as being far away. But the future is anything beyond *right now*. God is so powerful that He lives in the past, the present and the future all together! The Bible says that God's love never changes. God loved Adam and Eve in the beginning of time. He loves us today. And He will *always* love us and everyone He has created— for all of eternity!

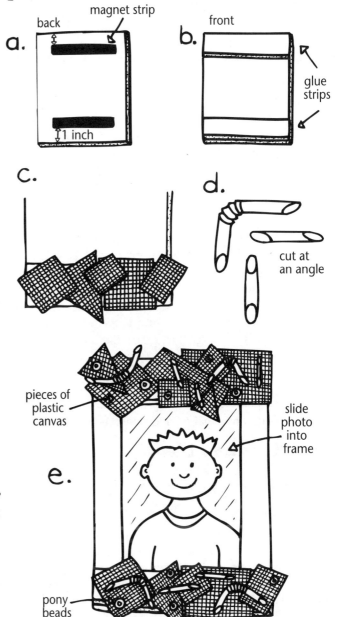

"Cross of Nails" Plaque (30–35 MINUTES)

Materials

- ❏ 1x6-inch (2.5x15-cm) pine boards
- ❏ metallic spray paint in gold and purple
- ❏ glossy black acrylic paint
- ❏ ¾-inch (1.9-cm) copper nails
- ❏ 20-gauge copper wire (available at home-improvement stores)
- ❏ aluminum screening (available at home-improvement stores)
- ❏ saw
- ❏ hammers
- ❏ wire cutters

For each child—
- ❏ one sawtooth picture hanger with nails
- ❏ two 4-inch (10-cm) nails
- ❏ two 7-inch (17.5-cm) nails

Standard Supplies

- ❏ scissors
- ❏ wide paintbrushes
- ❏ ruler
- ❏ shallow containers
- ❏ newspaper

Preparation

Use saw to cut pine boards into 10-inch (25-cm) lengths—one for each child. Cut copper wire into the following lengths: 12 inches (30 cm)—one for each child; 6 inches (15 cm)—four for each child; 2 inches (5 cm)—three for each child. Cut screening into 5x8-inch (12.5x 20-cm) rectangles—one for each child. Cover an outdoor area with newspaper and lightly paint 4- and 7-inch (10- and 17.5-cm) nails with purple metallic spray paint. Spray screen rectangles with gold paint. Pour black acrylic paint into shallow containers and cover work area with newspaper.

Instruct each child in the following procedures:

- Lay pine board vertically and nail sawtooth hanger ½ inch (1.25 cm) from the top, centering the hanger.
- Turn board over and paint the front and edges with black paint. Set aside to dry.
- Take the two 4-inch (10-cm) nails and place together so that there is a nail head at either end (sketch a).
- Keeping nail ends even, wrap a 6-inch (15-cm) length of copper wire around both nails, about 1 inch (2.5 cm) from each end. Twist and press the wire ends down.
- Take the two 7-inch (17.5-cm) nails and repeat procedure.
- Lay the 4-inch (10-cm) nails across the 7-inch (17.5-cm) nails to make a cross. Make sure all copper wire ends are on the back side of cross.
- Take one piece of 12-inch (30-cm) copper wire and wrap the intersection of the nails in one direction, making the first leg of an X. Then wrap in the other direction, forming the second leg of an X (sketch b).
- Fold screen in half vertically to find center.
- On back side of nail cross, thread a 2-inch (5-cm) wire under the wrapped wires at the top, center and bottom (sketch c).
- Center the nail cross on the screen and attach the ends of the 2-inch (5-cm) wires through the screen. Twist the wire ends together and press flat so that they are concealed. Trim, if necessary.
- Make a ¼-inch (.625-cm) fringe on the screen by removing some screen threads from along the edges (sketch d).
- Center screen vertically on the painted board. Hammer copper nails at the top and bottom center, about ½ inch (1.25 cm) from each edge. Smooth out any ripples in screen. Then hammer a copper nail into each of the four corners.
- Hammer additional nails along screen edges, spacing about 1 inch (2.5 cm) apart (sketch e).

Simplification Ideas

Pre-paint pine boards with black spray paint to shorten in-class craft time, or eliminate painting nails, screens and boards altogether.

Lab Notes

Jesus came to earth to tell us about God and show what God is like. Jesus also came to earth to die, but God's power raised Him back to life! It was all part of God's plan. Why did Jesus have to die? (He died to take the punishment for our sins. He died so that sin no longer keeps us separated from God.) **Now we can live forever with God if we believe that Jesus died for the wrong things we do. This cross plaque can remind you that Jesus' death made a way for us to be a part of God's family forever.**

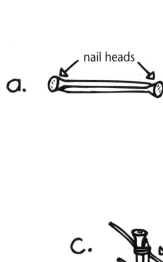

a.

nail heads

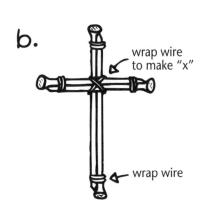

b.

wrap wire
to make "x"

wrap wire

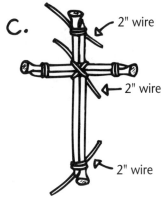

c.

2" wire

2" wire

2" wire

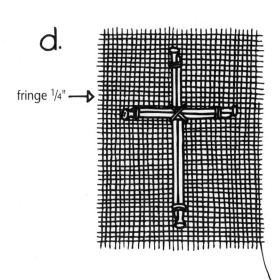

d.

fringe 1/4"

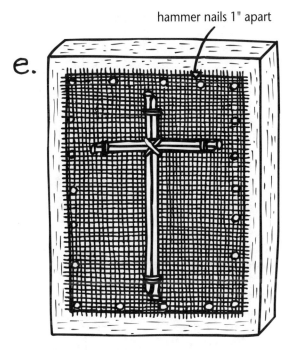

e.

hammer nails 1" apart

Wiry-Guys Poster (30–35 MINUTES)

Materials

- ❏ underground cable (available at home-improvement stores)
- ❏ black foamboard (available at craft stores) or mat board
- ❏ brightly colored corrugated paper (available at craft or school supply stores)
- ❏ paint pens in metallic colors
- ❏ nails
- ❏ wire cutters
- ❏ needle-nose pliers

For each child—
- ❏ one self-adhesive picture hanger

Standard Supplies

- ❏ Bible
- ❏ chalkboard and chalk or butcher paper and felt pen
- ❏ pencil
- ❏ glue
- ❏ scissors
- ❏ craft knife
- ❏ measuring stick

Preparation

Use wire cutters to cut cable into 36-inch (90-cm) lengths. Use craft knife to cut off the cover of cable to reveal the individual colored wires inside. Separate the wires—three differently colored wires for each child. Use craft knife to cut foamboard or mat board into 17x19-inch (42.5x47.5—cm) rectangles—one for each child. Cut corrugated paper into 1½-inch (3.75-cm) strips. Then cut strips into 19-inch (47.5-cm) lengths and 14-inch (35-cm) lengths—two of each length for each child. Letter Ephesians 5:2 on chalkboard or butcher paper for children's reference.

Instruct each child in the following procedures:

- Use one 36-inch (90-cm) wire to make an outline of a person. Bend the wire in half to find the midpoint. At midpoint, form a loop and twist wire together to make head and neck (sketch a).
- Bend remaining wire into a figure's outline and clothing—arms, hands, legs, feet, dress, etc. Use pliers, if needed. To keep figure's shape intact, twist wires together at different intervals—at ankles, wrists, waist or where wires intersect (sketch a). The Wiry Guy can be bent to show a motion, such as dancing, running, etc. (sketch b).
- Repeat procedure to make two more Wiry Guys out of remaining wires.
- Glue corrugated strips around the edge of foamboard or mat board to make a frame. Glue longer strips to longest sides of board. Glue shorter strips to shorter sides of board.
- Position your Wiry Guys on top of board, leaving space to letter the words of Ephesians 5:2.
- Use nail to poke a hole in board near the top and the bottom of each figure.
- Cut two 2-inch (5-cm) pieces of wire that match the color of one Wiry Guy. Wrap one wire around the neck of figure and then push both ends of wire through the hole to the back of board. Twist wires once and then flatten to the back (sketch c).
- In the same manner, use the second wire to attach Wiry Guy to board near bottom of figure.
- Attach the other two Wiry Guys to the board in the same manner.
- Use pencil to lightly letter words of the verse on the board. You may curve the verse to fit around the figures.
- Carefully trace over your letters with a paint pen. Allow paint to dry (sketch d).
- Apply a self-adhesive hanger to top center on back of board.

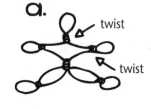

a. twist / twist

b.

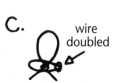

c. wire doubled

hole in front of board   back of board

Lab Notes

The Bible says, *Live a life of love, just as Christ loved us and gave himself up for us* **(Ephesians 5:2). When we know that Jesus loves us even though we aren't perfect, we will be more willing to love other people even though they aren't perfect. What did Jesus do that showed His love for us?** (He died for our sins.) **Jesus died to forgive the wrong things that we do. We can share His love with others when we forgive, too.**

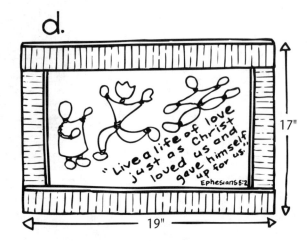

d.

17"

19"

"Take-Apart Art" Invention (30–45 MINUTES)

Materials

- ¼-inch (.625-cm) masonite pegboard (available at home-improvement stores)
- enamel spray paint in two or more bright colors
- ¼-inch (.625-cm) clear vinyl tubing—approximately 2 to 3 feet (.6 to .9 m) for each child (available at home-improvement stores)
- bell wire in assorted colors—approximately 5 feet (1.5 m) for each child (available at home-improvement stores)
- metal washers
- wing nuts
- old CDs
- brightly colored drinking straws
- translucent colored pony beads
- 1-inch (2.5-cm) paper fasteners
- circular saw
- several screw drivers
- several pliers
- heavy-duty scissors

For each child—
- a minimum of twelve 1- to 1½-inch (2.5- to 3.75-cm) machine screws or bolts
- twelve nuts—one to fit each screw or bolt

Standard Supplies

- measuring stick
- shallow containers
- newspaper

Preparation

Use saw to cut pegboard into 12x16-inch (30x40-cm) rectangles—one for each child. Spread newspaper in well-ventilated area and spray smooth side of boards with spray paint. Paint metal washers and wing nuts with a contrasting color of spray paint. Allow to dry. Cut bell wire and plastic tubing into 2-foot (.6-m) lengths. Place small items in separate shallow containers. Set out all other items.

Instruct each child in the following procedures:

- Decide what you want to create on the board with all the materials: a design, picture, a word or your name.
- Lay board on table painted side up. Arrange screws or bolts as desired by inserting through the back of pegboard through the holes.
- Place washers or CDs on screws or bolts. Screw nuts and/or wing nuts onto bolts to secure. Tighten with pliers and/or screw drivers if needed (sketch a).
- Cut plastic tubing and colored straws into short lengths. Thread tubing, straws and/or beads onto wires, if desired (sketch b).
- Wrap wire lengths around bolts to make designs or letters.
- Attach beads to board with paper fasteners (sketch b).
- Use the materials creatively to invent your own piece of art! You can take apart your art and change your design whenever you like!

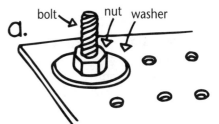

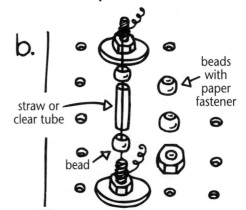

Simplification Ideas

For less preparation time, use pre-painted white pegboard. Leave board, washers and wing nuts unpainted.

Enrichment Ideas

The materials you may use are endless: any metal or plastic hardware may be used; and brightly colored paper, Fun Foam, plastic canvas or cellophane may be cut in shapes, punched with a hole punch and then attached to board.

Lab Notes

God made people to be creative! Inventors create unusual things out of ordinary objects. Almost 60 years ago an engineer was working on a Navy ship when a metal spring came loose and flip-flopped on the floor. The man remembered how funny the spring looked. When he got home, he made a tightly coiled spring out of a long piece of metal. He called the new toy a Slinky and they've been sold in toy stores ever since!

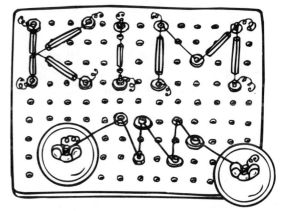

Creation Wire Sculpture (TWO-DAY CRAFT/20–30 MINUTES EACH DAY)

Materials

- ❏ Creation Patterns (p.68)
- ❏ fiberglass or wire window screening (available at home-improvement stores)
- ❏ clear Con-Tact paper
- ❏ fabric paints in various colors including metallic and iridescent colors
- ❏ 18-gauge copper wire (available at home-improvement stores)
- ❏ self-hardening clay, Play-Doh or modeling clay
- ❏ permanent felt pens
- ❏ rubbing alcohol
- ❏ toothpicks
- ❏ needle-nose pliers
- ❏ wire cutters

Optional—
- ❏ shredded mylar gift filler
- ❏ glue

For each child—
- ❏ one spray paint can cap (or similar plastic cap) or small clay pot

Standard Supplies

- ❏ photocopier
- ❏ copier paper
- ❏ pencils
- ❏ scissors
- ❏ thin paintbrushes
- ❏ ruler
- ❏ paper towels

Day One Preparation

Cut window screening and Con-Tact paper into 8x10-inch (20x25-cm) rectangles—one of each for each child. Photocopy Creation Patterns onto paper—one copy for each child.

Instruct each child in the following procedures:

- Peel backing off Con-Tact paper and with partner's help, apply to window screen rectangle. Press down and smooth out any bubbles.
- Decide which creations you want in your sculpture. You may want only one type such as flowers in different colors or just stars, moon and sun. Or you may choose a variety of creations.
- Lay photocopy under window screen with Con-Tact paper side up. With a permanent felt pen, trace five to eight symbols onto Con-Tact paper.
- Turn window screen over and paint shapes onto screen with fabric paint. Outline the shapes with the paint and then brush paint inward to fill in the shape. Continue adding small amounts of paint onto shape and spreading with brush as needed (sketch a).
- After using each paint color, clean the paintbrush with a paper towel dampened with alcohol.
- Allow screen to dry overnight.

Day Two Preparation

Cut wire into 8- to 12-inch (20- to 30-cm) lengths—eleven for each child.

Instruct each child in the following procedures:

- Cut out screen shapes. Do not peel off Con-Tact paper.
- Use permanent pens to add any details to screen side of shapes (sketch b).
- Use toothpick to poke a hole near the bottom and the top of each shape.
- Insert a wire through the bottom hole of shape, entering from the screen front. Then thread through the top hole. Use pliers or fingers to bend end of wire into a U shape to keep wire in place. Repeat process for each remaining shape (sketch c).
- Wrap some wire stems around pencils or toothpicks to make wires spiral (sketch d).
- Reserve one of the remaining wires for later use. Then use pliers to curl the ends of the remaining wire lengths (sketch e).
- Hold all wires together and wrap with the reserved wire length about 2 inches (5 cm) from wire ends. Use pliers to curl the ends of the wrapping wire (sketch f).
- Press clay or Play-Doh into the spray paint cap or clay pot to make sculpture base. Insert bound wire ends into center. (Optional: Glue or press confetti or shredded mylar into the clay or Play-Doh to cover.) Arrange wires to make an artistic display. Face screen side of shapes to the front. Bend and curve wires to make shapes fan out (sketch g).

Lab Notes

What does the Bible say God created first? (Light.) **Before God created light, everything was in darkness. Because God knew that life needs light, that's what He made first. Every living thing depends on light to survive. What other creations are you glad God included in our world? What part of creation would you miss most if it suddenly disappeared?**

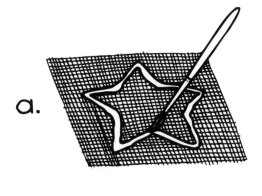

a.

b.

add details with pen

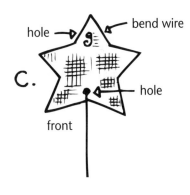

c.

hole

bend wire

hole

front

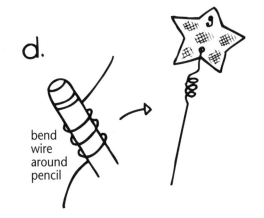

d.

bend wire around pencil

e.

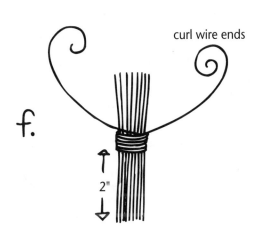

f.

curl wire ends

2"

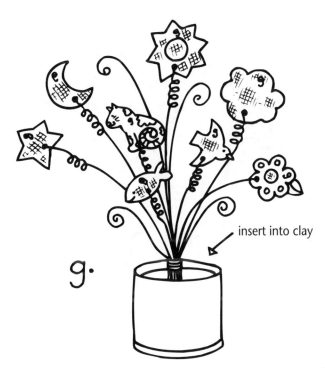

g.

insert into clay

Creation Patterns

CD Spinner (35–45 MINUTES)

Materials
- ❏ plastic canvas in various colors
- ❏ colorful drinking straws
- ❏ pony beads
- ❏ neon-colored nylon twine
- ❏ brightly colored plastic lacing

For each child—
- ❏ two old CDs
- ❏ one large fishing swivel
- ❏ one small fishing swivel

Standard Supplies
- ❏ scissors
- ❏ ruler

Preparation
Cut plastic canvas into 7x9-inch (17.5x22.5-cm) rectangles—one for each child. Cut out an angled arch 5½ inches (13.75 cm) wide and 4 inches (10 cm) high (sketch a) from the center of each rectangle. Cut additional colors of plastic canvas into 1x6-inch (2.5x15-cm) strips—four for each child. Save canvas scraps for decorating spinners. Cut twine into 7-inch (17.5-cm) and 12-inch (30-cm) lengths—two of each length for each child. Cut straws into 1-inch (2.5-cm) pieces.

Instruct each child in the following procedures:

- Place CDs together with the printed sides facing each other.
- Thread a 7-inch (17.5-cm) length of twine through the center of the two CDs and then through the loop of smaller swivel. Knot ends together and then trim. Open the hook of the swivel and fasten to the bottom center of the arch (sketch b).
- Fasten hook of large swivel to the center top edge of the plastic canvas.
- Thread another 7-inch (17.5-cm) length of twine through the loop end of large swivel and knot ends together to make hanger (sketch b). Trim ends.
- Cut plastic canvas scraps into small shapes to decorate the arch. Attach shapes, or several layers of shapes, to the arch by weaving plastic lacing through holes. String pony beads and short pieces of drinking straws onto lacing to add interest. Make large knots in the ends of lacing and trim ends (sketch c). Repeat on back side of canvas.
- Hang four canvas strips from the bottom edges of the arch. Make a large knot in one end of a 12-inch (30-cm) length of twine and thread on a pony bead. Weave twine through the top 2 inches (5 cm) of one narrow canvas strip.
- Attach strip to canvas arch by weaving twine across bottom edge of one side of arch. Continue to weave twine through top 2 inches (5 cm) of a second canvas strip.
- Thread a bead onto twine and secure with a large knot. Adjust strips to hang evenly and freely from bottom edge of arch (sketch d).
- Repeat procedure to attach two plastic canvas strips to the other side of arch opening.

Lab Notes
Music is recorded on compact discs (CDs) using lasers. Lasers are beams of light that are a million times hotter and brighter than sunlight. Bursts of laser light make tiny pits in the disc. When you play a music CD, a laser beam in the CD player reflects off the pits as the disc spins. These reflections make sound you can hear. Lasers are used to do many incredible things. What are some things lasers are used for? (Surgery. Fiber optics in televisions and telephones. Scanners in grocery stores.) **God cares about us so much He created people who can invent things that help us.**

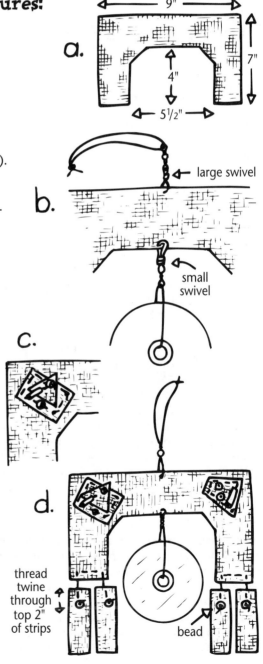

Door Dangler (30–45 MINUTES)

Materials

- black fiberglass screening (available at home-improvement stores)
- ¼-inch (.625-cm) clear vinyl tubing (available at home-improvement stores)
- 16-gauge copper wire (available at home-improvement stores)
- plastic lacing string (available at craft stores)
- lightweight clear vinyl sheeting (available at fabric stores)
- pony beads
- metallic chenille wires
- 24-gauge beading wire (available at craft stores)
- large sequin stars
- 20-mm sequin bangles
- jump rings
- several needle-nose pliers
- wire cutters

Standard Supplies

- brightly colored paper
- felt pens in various colors
- scissors
- hole punch
- measuring stick

Preparation

Prepare the following for each child: One 4x10-inch (10x25-cm) rectangle of fiberglass screening. One 10½-inch (26.25-cm) length of vinyl tubing. One 13-inch (32.5-cm) length of copper wire. One 24-inch (60-cm) length of lacing string. One 3-inch (7.5-cm) square of colored paper. One 4-inch (10-cm) vinyl square that has three holes punched on each side (sketch a).

Instruct each child in the following procedures:

- Insert copper wire through clear tubing.
- To make handle, insert each end of copper wire through the upper corners of screen, ¼-inch (.625-cm) away from each edge. Thread a bead on each end. Using pliers, curl the wire ends to secure beads to wire (sketch b).
- With felt pen, write "Jesus is the Way" on paper square. Cut around the words to make any shape (star, curved, jagged, heart, etc.) or leave it square.
- Place paper on the center of the beaded side of screen. Lay the vinyl square over the paper. Weave the plastic lacing through the holes in vinyl square and screen. String some beads onto lacing as you work. Where ends of lacing meet, tie ends together in a knot (sketch c). Trim ends.
- Decorate the screen. Thread beads on two chenille wires and then bend into flat shapes. Cut short lengths of beading wire and use to secure chenille wire shapes to screen (sketch d).
- Attach jump rings to bangle sequins and then attach jump rings to screen. Wrap beading wire around sequin star to secure to screen.
- Cut short lengths of copper wire and attach to screen or chenille wires. Curl the ends with pliers.

Lab Notes

Jesus came to make a way for us to be with God. In the Bible, Jesus says, *I am the way and the truth and the life. No one comes to the Father except through me. If you really knew me, you would know my Father as well* (John 14:6,7). God sent Jesus to connect us to Him and to show us what God is like. How would you describe Jesus? No one has seen God, but we can know that God is also (characteristics children named) because people got to see, hear and be with Jesus.

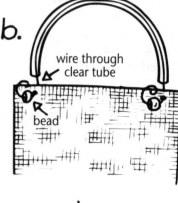

punch holes in vinyl

a.

b.

wire through clear tube

bead

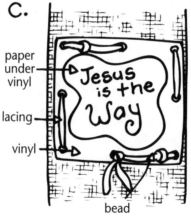

c.

paper under vinyl

lacing

vinyl

bead

d.

large sequin bangles with jump ring

star sequin

beads

chenille wires attached with wire

wire embellishment

70

© 2000 by Gospel Light. Permission to photocopy granted. *Discovery Lab Crafts for Kids*

Section Four
Bonus Pages

"Comet the Cat" Paper Bag Puppet

Use the instructions and patterns for the Comet the Cat Puppet to make your own lab cat for prekindergarten and kindergarten children to enjoy.

GP4U Crafts Section

GP4U stands for "God's Plan for You." This craft section includes fun, colorful projects that will reinforce the message of God's plan of salvation for each child. A symbol represents each part of God's plan and all are used in creating these crafts. You may want to reproduce a copy of "Do You Know About GP4U?" (p. 75) for each child. In years to come, children will remember God's plan for them and how much He loves them!

GP4U Time Capsule

Have each child make his or her own time capsule to encapsulate what they've learned about God and what they are like at the time of your VBS. Use the GP4U Time Capsule craft instructions and reproducible From Time to Time page found in the "GP4U Crafts Section." Children complete the "Today" portion of the page and place it into their time capsule. Children may put their *Student Newspapers* from VBS in the time capsule. Also encourage children to bring in other small items from home to place inside capsule: small items they collect, photos of themselves and family or friends, newspaper clippings, pictures they've drawn, etc. Children keep their time capsules sealed until a designated time in the future (six months, a year, five years, etc.) when they open them.

Bible Memory Verse Coloring Posters

The Bible Memory Verse Coloring Posters contain five Bible Memory Verse designs for younger elementary children and five for older elementary children. Here are several ideas for using these pages:

- Use the photocopied pages as awards for children who memorize the Bible verse. They may take the page home to color and display.
- Photocopy a set of coloring posters for each student. Cover with a folded sheet of construction paper and staple to make a coloring book.
- Use the pages in class for transition times or for students who finish an activity ahead of other students.
- Play a coloring game. Place a variety of felt pens on the table. Recite the verse together. Then each student may choose a pen and use it to color on his or her page for one minute. When time is up, students put pens down and repeat verse together again. Students then choose another pen and color for one minute. Repeat process until pages are completed or students tire of activity.
- Customize the pages by covering the Bible verse with white paper and lettering another verse or saying in its place before you photocopy.

Student Certificates and Awards

The awards and certificates on the following pages may be personalized for various uses. Just follow these simple procedures:

1. Tear out certificate and letter the name of your program on the appropriate line.
2. Photocopy as many copies of certificate as needed.
3. Letter each child's certificate with his or her name (and achievement when appropriate).

Sticker Posters

1. Photocopy a sticker poster for each student.
2. After students color posters, attach them to a wall or bulletin board.
3. Students add stickers to their posters each day as they arrive. Or you may want to use stickers as rewards for reciting Bible memory verses, being helpful or completing assignments.

"Comet the Cat" Paper Bag Puppet

Materials

- ❏ Cat Puppet Patterns
- ❏ wide gift wrap ribbon
- ❏ one paper lunch bag
- ❏ three buttons

Optional—
- ❏ two large wiggle eyes
- ❏ yarn for fur and whiskers
- ❏ one Velcro round

Standard Supplies

- ❏ photocopier
- ❏ white card stock
- ❏ craft glue
- ❏ felt pens in various colors
- ❏ scissors
- ❏ ruler

Instructions:

- Photocopy Cat Puppet Patterns onto white card stock.
- Color patterns with felt pens. Cut out.
- With the bag folded, glue the cat's head to flap of paper bag (sketch a).
- Glue the cat's body below the head on the bag (sketch a).
- On the back side of pocket, squeeze a line of glue along the sides and bottom, leaving the top unglued, and glue to lab coat (sketch b).
- Glue three buttons on coat.
- Knot a 6-inch (15-cm) piece of ribbon in the middle to make a bow tie. Trim ends to make even. Glue under cat's head (sketch c).
- Place magnifying glass in lab coat pocket.
- *Optional:* Glue on yarn for fur and whiskers. Glue on wiggle eyes. Remove backing from both sides of Velcro round; attach loop side to the front of one paw and hook side to back of magnifying glass handle, so puppet can "hold" magnifying glass.
- To make puppet "talk," slide hand inside paper bag. Open and close hand in flap of bag.

a.

glue to flap

glue to bag

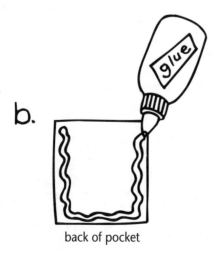

b.

glue

back of pocket

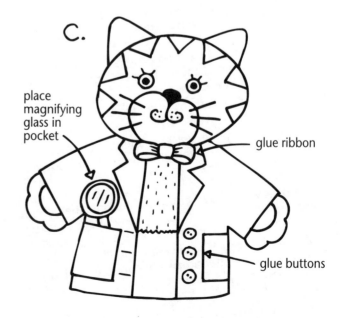

c.

place magnifying glass in pocket

glue ribbon

glue buttons

Cat Puppet Patterns

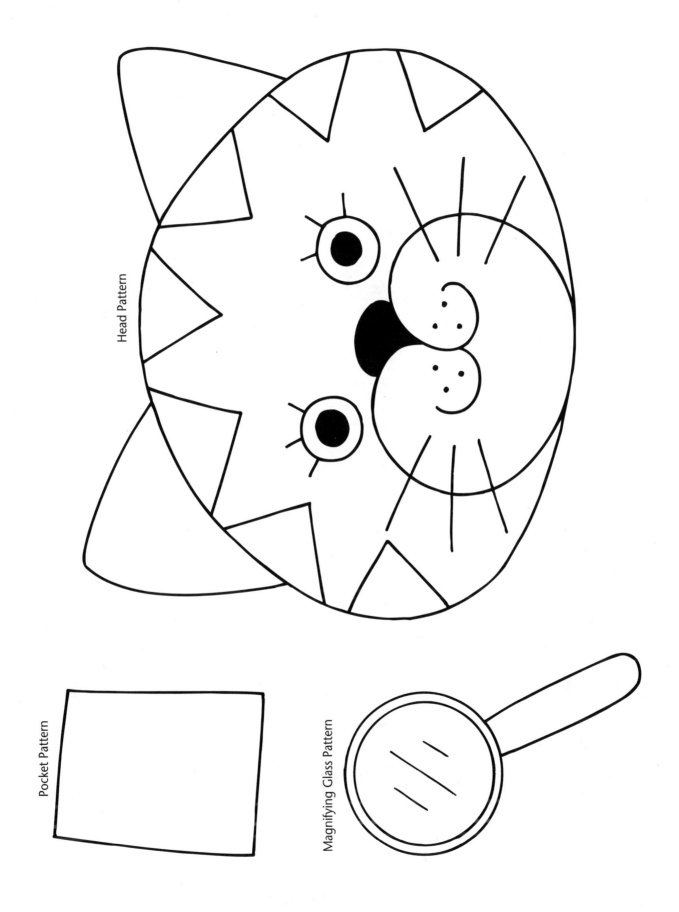

Head Pattern

Pocket Pattern

Magnifying Glass Pattern

Cat Puppet Patterns

glue pocket here

Body Pattern

Do You Know About GP4U?

GP4U stands for "God's Plan for You." You can remember God's plan by remembering five easy symbols and what they represent. Then you can spread the word about GP4U to others!

yellow sun

The God who made the universe created you and loves you.

gray/ blue cloud

Sin has separated us from God.

red heart

God loved us so much He sent His Son, Jesus, so we can know what God is like.

purple cross

Jesus died and rose again so that you can receive forgiveness for your sins and be a member of God's family.

green fish

You can live as God's child and show His love to others.

GP4U Time Capsule (20–25 MINUTES)

Materials

❑ From Time to Time page (p. 00)
❑ silver spray paint
❑ primer or flat black spray paint
❑ paint pens or permanent felt pens in bright colors including yellow, blue, red, purple and green
❑ cellophane in various colors

For each child—
❑ one potato chip canister with lid

Standard Supplies

❑ photocopier
❑ brightly colored copier paper
❑ pencils
❑ glue sticks
❑ scissors
❑ newspaper
❑ ruler

Preparation

Photocopy From Time to Time page onto brightly colored paper—one copy for each child. Cut cellophane into pieces about 5 inches (12.5 cm) square. Cover table or floor in well-ventilated area with newspaper. Set potato chip canisters on newspaper and spray with primer or flat black paint to cover label printing. Then spray with silver paint to cover completely. Allow to dry.

Instruct each child in the following procedures:

- Cut different shapes from colored cellophane (small triangles, squares, etc.) or cut small GP4U shapes (sun, cloud, heart, cross, fish).
- Use glue stick to apply cellophane shapes to decorate canister (see sketch).
- Use paint pens or permanent felt pens to draw GP4U symbols or other designs such as dots, squiggles, lines, etc. (see sketch).
- On the plastic lid use paint or felt pens to write the date.
- Use pencil to write on From Time to Time paper, filling in the "Today" part. Leave the "In the Future" section blank.
- Put From Time to Time sheet in the time capsule, along with other items that represent what you are like and some things that are happening at the present time.

Lab Notes

Keep your time capsule sealed until a later date—(six months, a year, five years, etc.) from now. Then open your time capsule to remember what you were like and what you knew about God's plan for you in the year (2000). It will be fun to fill in your "From Time to Time" paper in the future and see how you have grown and changed. God's love for you will never change. He is the same today as He was in the beginning. And He will love you just as much in the future. God's plan is for all time!

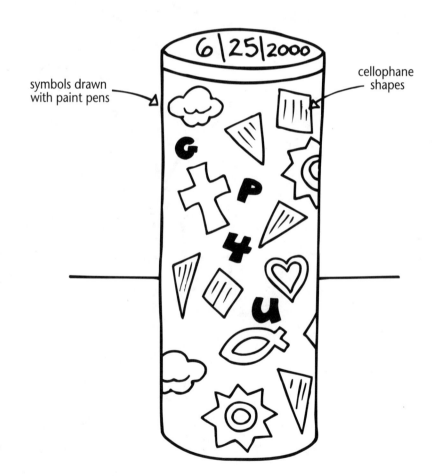

symbols drawn with paint pens

cellophane shapes

From Time to Time

Today	In the Future (fill in later)
My age:	
My favorite thing to do:	
My favorite person:	
I like the way I:	
Something I'd like to do someday:	
Something I've recently learned about God:	
I show God to other people when I:	

GP4U Disc Mobile (25–30 MINUTES)

<table>
<tr><td>

Materials

❑ silver thread or thin cord
For each child—
❑ two old CDs
❑ two silver chenille wires
❑ yellow, gray/blue, red, purple and green chenille wires (one each)

</td><td>

Standard Supplies

❑ scissors
❑ ruler

</td><td>

Preparation

For each child, cut lengths of thread as follows: two 12 inches (30 cm) long, two 9 inches (22.5 cm) long and one 6 inches (15 cm) long. Cut half of the silver chenille wires into 6-inch (15-cm) lengths—two lengths for each child.

</td></tr>
</table>

Instruct each child in the following procedures:

- Hold the 6-inch (15-cm) silver chenille wires together and bend in half to find the middle.

- Take the long silver chenille wire and bend in half to find the middle. Then hook the midpoint of the shorter wires over the midpoint of the long wire. Twist the long wire around the shorter wires to secure (sketch a).

- Stack the two CDs together with the printed sides facing each other.

- Insert the longer doubled chenille wire through the holes in CDs. Twist the top ends together and spread slightly apart to make hanging loop (sketch b).

- Turn CDs over and spread the shorter chenille wires apart evenly to lie flat against disc. Bend the ends of wires to the top side of discs to secure (sketch c).

- Form the GP4U symbols out of remaining chenille wires. Make the sun using one long yellow wire. Bend the long wire into a zig-zag pattern, making about seven peaks. Curve into a sun shape and twist wire ends together (sketch d).

- Form a fish using a green chenille wire. Curve wire and twist ends together about 1 inch (2.5 cm) from the ends to form fish tail (sketch d).

- Form heart using a red chenille wire. Twist ends together to form a circle and then form circle into a heart shape (sketch d).

- Form a cloud using a gray/blue chenille wire. Twist ends together to make a circle and then bend circle into several curved edges to make cloud shape (sketch d).

- Form a cross using a purple chenille wire. Twist ends together. Then form a long, thin rectangle. About 1 inch (2.5 cm) from top and bend wire out to sides and form the outline of the cross piece (sketch e).

- Tie the 6-inch (15-cm) length of thread to the sun shape. Then slide the opposite end of thread under one of the silver wire arms on underside of mobile. Tie end to one of the silver wires in the center of disc (sketch f). Sun will hang in the center.

- Tie the remaining threads to the remaining shapes.

- Then tie the opposite ends of threads to the silver wires near the disc edge. You may unbend the wires and then bend back over discs once thread is tied and knotted. Tie the shapes with same-length threads opposite each other to balance (sketch g).

- Trim thread ends.

Enrichment Idea

Follow directions for Crystal Cross craft (p. 30) and place all five chenille symbol shapes in borax and water solution overnight. Crystals will cover the chenille wires to make glittering ornaments. Then assemble mobile as instructed.

Lab Notes

What do all the symbols mean in GP4U? (Children review symbols and their meanings.) **The fish was a symbol that Christians used after Jesus came back to life. It was called an *Ichthus* (ICK-THOOS), the Greek word for fish, and was used as a secret code among people who followed Jesus. Many people didn't like what the early Christians believed and wanted them killed. So when Christians met each other, they would draw a fish to show they were Christians. Then they knew they were safe to talk freely. If the other person didn't understand or didn't draw a fish, a Christian knew he might be in danger. Even today, there are places in the world where people are in danger because they worship Jesus. We are fortunate that here we can talk freely about God's love and His Son, Jesus.**

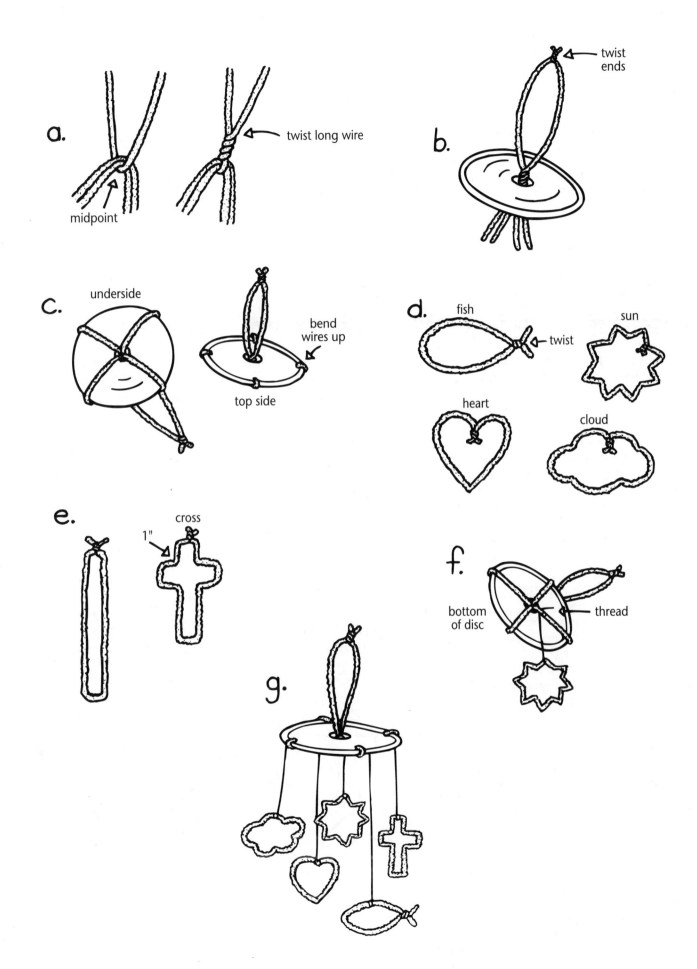

a. twist long wire
midpoint

b. twist ends

c. underside
bend wires up
top side

d. fish
twist
sun
heart
cloud

e. cross
1"

f. bottom of disc
thread

g.

GP4U Key Chain (30–35 MINUTES)

Materials
- GP4U Cover and Small Symbol Patterns
- Fun Foam in yellow, red, gray/blue, purple, green and one or two other colors (*Note:* Precut Fun Foam GP4U shapes are available from Gospel Light in the year 2000 only.)
- ball chain (found with lamp supplies)
- heavy-duty scissors or wire cutters

For each child—
- one ball chain connector (found with lamp supplies)

Standard Supplies
- lightweight cardboard
- pencils or pens
- thin-tip felt pens in various colors
- craft glue
- scissors
- several hole punches
- ruler

Preparation
With heavy-duty scissors or wire cutters, cut ball chain into 6-inch (15-cm) lengths—one for each child. Attach a connector to one end of each chain (sketch a). Trace several copies of GP4U Cover Pattern and each GP4U Small Symbol Pattern onto lightweight cardboard and cut out. Punch holes on all patterns where indicated on original pattern.

Instruct each child in the following procedures:

- Trace the GP4U symbol patterns onto the following colors of Fun Foam: sun—yellow, cloud—gray/blue, heart—red, cross—purple, fish—green. Mark the center of punched hole on each shape. Cut out shapes.
- Trace the cover pattern twice onto any color of Fun Foam. Mark the center of punched hole on Fun Foam. Cut out.
- Use hole punch to punch a hole in each shape where you marked. Save hole-punched circles.
- With felt pens, outline shapes and/or draw details on each shape.
- On one cover, use felt pen to write "GP4U."
- Glue punched foam circles on cover to decorate (sketch b).
- Assemble the symbols in GP4U order: sun on top and then cloud, heart, cross and fish. Align all the holes. Then place the decorated cover on top and the plain cover on the bottom (sketch c).
- Thread the chain through all holes in foam pieces and attach free end to the connector (sketch d).

Lab Notes
You can use your GP4U Key Chain for your house key or you can attach it to your backpack. However you decide to use it, your GP4U Key Chain can always remind you of God's love. What is God's plan for you? (Children review the symbol meanings.) **Now that you know God's plan from beginning to end, you may want to share it with a friend or someone you know who could use some good news. There are many people who'd like to know that God has a plan for their lives, too!**

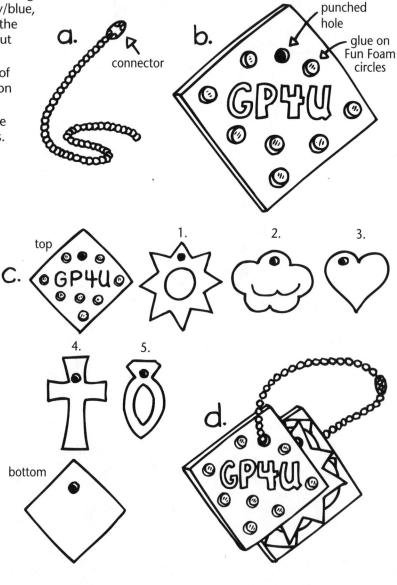

GP4U Cover and Small Symbol Patterns

GP4U Balance (30–35 MINUTES)

Materials
❏ GP4U Large Symbol Patterns
❏ Fun Foam in green, purple, red, yellow and gray/blue (*Note:* Precut Fun Foam GP4U shapes are available from Gospel Light in the year 2000 only.)
❏ 16-gauge copper wire (available at home-improvement stores)
❏ jump rings (available in jewelry section of craft stores)
❏ electrical tape in various colors
❏ high-tack adhesive (such as E-6000 or Goop)
❏ several needle-nose pliers
❏ wire cutters
For each child—
❏ two large, empty thread spools
❏ two 1½-inch (3.75-cm) metal washers
❏ one drinking straw

Standard Supplies
❏ lightweight cardboard
❏ pens
❏ scissors
❏ hole punch
❏ measuring stick

Preparation
Cut wire into 11-inch (27.5-cm) lengths and 21-inch (52.5-cm) lengths—one of each length for each child. For each 21-inch (52.5-cm) wire, use pliers to make small U-shaped crimps about 6 inches (15 cm) from each end of wire and then bend a small, open loop at one end (sketch a). Trace Large Symbol Patterns onto lightweight cardboard to make two or three copies of each pattern and then cut out.

Instruct each child in the following procedures:

- Wrap strips of electrical tape around each thread spool.
- Use adhesive to glue spools together. Then glue one washer on top of stacked spools and one washer on the bottom to dd weight (sketch b).
- Trace the symbol patterns onto the following colors of Fun Foam: sun—yellow, cloud—gray/blue, heart—red, cross—purple, fish—green. Cut out shapes.
- Punch a hole near top edge of each shape and insert a jump ring through each hole. Close jump rings with pliers.
- Gently bend the long wire into an arc shape.
- Insert the jump ring of the sun in the open loop. Pinch the loop closed with pliers.
- Thread the cloud onto wire to rest in the crimp next to the sun.
- Thread the jump ring of the cross onto the arc wire to rest in remaining crimp.
- With pliers, bend a small loop in the end of the arc wire. Insert the jump ring of the fish and pinch the loop closed with pliers.
- With pliers, make a medium-sized open loop in one end of the short wire.
- Insert jump ring of the heart into the loop.
- Insert the midpoint of the arc wire inside the loop. Pinch the loop closed with pliers (sketch c).
- Place the drinking straw in the center hole of the spool base. Place the end of the shorter wire in the drinking straw/spool base (sketch d).
- Carefully adjust the arc to balance.

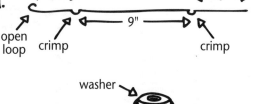

a. ←6"→   ←6"→
open loop   crimp   9"   crimp

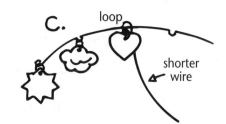

b. washer   electrical tape   washer

c. loop   shorter wire

Lab Notes
What does the red heart represent in God's plan? (Jesus came to show God's love.) **Our whole calendar is based on when Jesus came. Every date before Jesus is labeled B.C., which means "before Christ." Every date after Jesus' birth is A.D., which stands for *anno Domini*—this is Latin for "in the year of the Lord." Jesus' coming is so important that He is the center of the history of our world. This balance can remind you that Jesus' love is also the center of God's plan for you.**

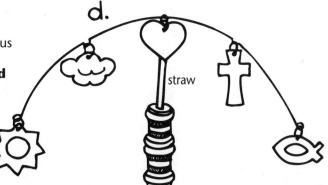

d. straw

GP4U Large Symbol Patterns

GP4U Sky Spiral (30–35 MINUTES)

Materials

❏ GP4U Large Symbol Patterns (p. 83)
❏ Spiral Pattern
❏ sheets of Fun Foam in yellow, gray/blue, red, purple, green (*Note:* Precut Fun Foam GP4U shapes are available from Gospel Light in the year 2000 only.)
❏ colored plastic lacing

For each child—

❏ one 9x12-inch (22.5x30-cm) sheet of Fun Foam (a different color from the colors listed above)
❏ six pony beads

Standard Supplies

❏ lightweight cardboard
❏ pencil
❏ pens
❏ scissors
❏ hole punches
❏ measuring stick

Preparation

Trace GP4U Large Symbol Patterns onto lightweight cardboard to make one or two copies of each pattern. Cut out. Trace the outside of Spiral Pattern onto the individual sheets of Fun Foam—one for each child. Following the example on the Spiral Pattern, use a pencil to draw a spiral on each circle. Mark holes on each spiral where indicated on pattern. Cut plastic lacing into 8-inch (20-cm) lengths—five for each child. Cut lacing into 14-inch (35-cm) lengths—one for each child.

Instruct each child in the following procedures:

- Trace the symbol patterns onto the following colors of Fun Foam: sun—yellow, cloud—gray/blue, heart—red, cross—purple, fish—green. Cut out shapes.
- Cut out spiral along lines.
- Use a hole punch to punch holes in spiral where marked and in the top of each symbol shape.
- Thread a pony bead onto the 14-inch (35-cm) length of lacing and pull ends even. From the underside of spiral, thread ends through the hole in the spiral center. Tie lacing ends together to make hanger; trim ends (sketch a).
- Attach the GP4U symbols to the spiral as follows: Thread an 8-inch (20-cm) length of lacing through the hole in the sun shape. Pull lacing ends even. Entering from the underside of spiral, thread ends through the hole closest to the center of the spiral. Slide a pony bead onto the doubled lacing; then tie lacing ends in a knot and trim ends (sketch b).
- In the same manner, attach remaining shapes to spiral in GP4U order (cloud, heart, cross, fish), working from the center of spiral to the outer end (sketch c).

Lab Notes

Review the meaning of GP4U symbols by saying, **Think of the top of your spiral as "In the beginning...." Where did God's plan begin?** (God created the earth. He created us.) **Then what happened?** (Adam and Eve sinned. Sin separates us from God.) **Then what did God do?** (He sent Jesus to show His love.) **How did Jesus bring us back to God?** (He took the punishment for our sin by dying on the cross. Then He came back to life.) **So now what do we do?** (If we believe in Jesus and what He did for us, we can be God's children. We can show His love to other people.)

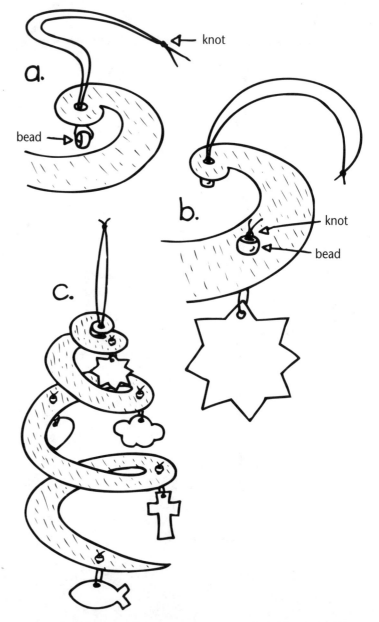

84

Spiral Pattern

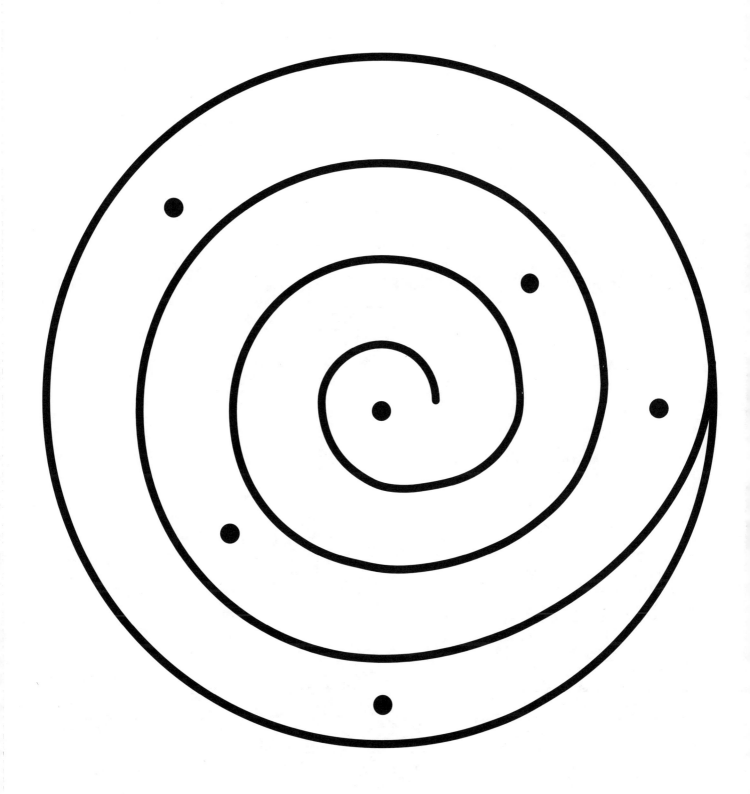

GP4U Cube (25–30 MINUTES)

Materials
- ❑ GP4U Large Symbol Patterns (p. 83)
- ❑ Fun Foam in yellow, gray/blue, red, purple, green and one other color (*Note:* Precut Fun Foam GP4U shapes are available from Gospel Light in the year 2000 only.)
- ❑ fine-tip fabric paints in various colors

For each child—
- ❑ one white folded 4-inch (10-cm) square gift box (available in giftwrap section of stationery or craft stores)

Standard Supplies
- ❑ lightweight cardboard
- ❑ pens
- ❑ craft glue
- ❑ scissors

Preparation
Trace GP4U Large Symbol Patterns onto lightweight cardboard to make one or two copies of each pattern; then cut out.

Instruct each child in the following procedures:

- Trace the symbol patterns onto the following colors of Fun Foam: sun—yellow, cloud—gray/blue, heart—red, cross—purple, fish—green. Cut out shapes.
- Assemble box and close lid.
- Use the bottom of the box as a pattern and trace two squares on the additional color of Fun Foam (sketch a). Cut out squares.
- Glue one square onto the bottom of box and one square onto the top lid of box. Press down to make sure Fun Foam is glued down well.
- Glue the Fun Foam symbols to the four sides of box and one on the top lid (sketch b).
- Use fabric paint to write "GP4U" on box and, if desired, decorate with dots, squiggles and other details (sketch c). Allow to dry several hours or overnight.

Simplification Idea
Eliminate decorating with fabric paint.

Lab Notes
You can use your GP4U Cube to store treasures. Or you could place a small gift or treat inside your box and give it to someone to show God's love. How did God show His love for us? (He created us. He sent Jesus to take the punishment for our sins. He made a way so that we can be with Him forever.) **When we know how much God loves us, we will want others to know about His love, too.**

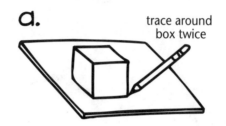

a. trace around box twice

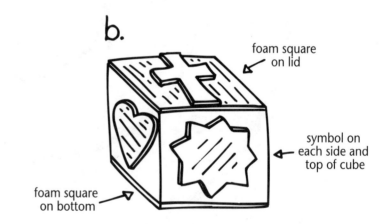

b. foam square on lid
symbol on each side and top of cube
foam square on bottom

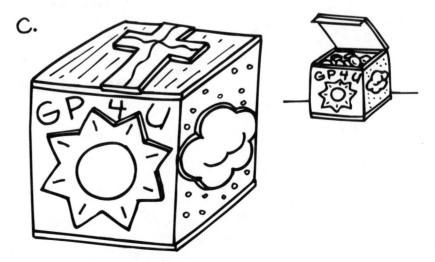

c.

GP4U Bracelet or Choker (15–20 MINUTES)

Materials
❑ black cording
❑ fine-tip paint pens in yellow, gray/blue, purple and green
❑ red heart-shaped plastic beads
❑ pony beads

For each child—
❑ four white 12-mm wooden beads in square, barrel or round shapes (*Note:* GP4U pre-painted beads are available from Gospel Light in the year 2000 only. If purchased, eliminate paint pens, heart beads and wooden beads from materials.)

Standard Supplies
❑ transparent tape
❑ scissors
❑ measuring stick

Preparation
Cut cording into 14-inch (35-cm) lengths for bracelets and 20-inch (50-cm) lengths for chokers—one bracelet or choker length for each child.

Instruct each child in the following procedures:

- With paint pens, draw a yellow sun, gray/blue cloud, purple cross and green fish on four white wooden beads—one symbol on each bead. Allow to dry. Then paint the same symbols on the opposite sides of beads (sketch a).
- Wrap one end of cording tightly with tape to make threading needle (sketch b).
- String one pony bead on cord.
- Then string on the fish bead, cross bead, a heart bead, the cloud bead, the sun bead and one more pony bead (sketch c).
- Adjust the beads so that they are centered in the middle of the cord. Knot the cord close to each pony bead on either side of larger beads to hold beads in place.
- Remove the tape from end of cord. Knot each end of cord to keep cord from unraveling.
- Ask a friend to tie your bracelet or choker on you. You may be able to slip your bracelet off and on, if tied loosely.

Simplification Idea
For younger children, teacher decorates beads with symbols before class time.

Lab Notes
You can wear your bracelet/choker to remember God's plan for you. Some-day you may want to give it to someone whom you would like to tell about God's love. What does the sun represent in God's plan? Review all GP4U symbol meanings with children.

a.

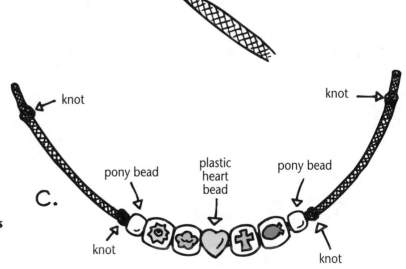

b. wrap tape

c. knot   knot
pony bead   plastic heart bead   pony bead
knot   knot

GP4U Backpack Clip (15–20 MINUTES)

Materials
- ❏ black cording
- ❏ fine-tip paint pens in yellow, gray/blue, purple and green
- ❏ red heart-shaped plastic beads
- ❏ pony beads

For each child—
- ❏ four white 12-mm wooden beads in square, barrel or round shapes (*Note:* GP4U pre-painted beads are available from Gospel Light in the year 2000 only. If purchased, eliminate paint pens, heart beads and wooden beads from materials.)
- ❏ one lanyard clip (available at craft stores)

Standard Supplies
- ❏ transparent tape
- ❏ scissors
- ❏ ruler

Preparation
Cut cording into 12-inch (30-cm) lengths—one for each child.

Instruct each child in the following procedures:

- With paint pens, draw a yellow sun, gray/blue cloud, purple cross and green fish on four white wooden beads—one symbol on each bead. Allow to dry. Then paint the same symbols on the opposite sides of beads (sketch a).
- Thread cord through lanyard clip and knot the center of cord to the clip (sketch b).
- Holding ends of cord even, tightly wrap the ends with tape to make a threading needle (sketch c).
- String one pony bead onto cord.
- Then string on the sun bead, cloud bead, a heart bead, the cross bead, the fish bead and one more pony bead (sketch d).
- Double knot the cord ends together near the last pony bead to secure beads in place.
- Remove tape from cord ends.

Simplification Idea
For younger children, teacher decorates beads with symbols before class time.

Lab Notes
You can attach your GP4U clip to your backpack or sports bag. You can attach it to a key ring. Or you could give it to someone with whom you'd like to share God's love. God's plan includes us. He wants us to spread His love to other people. What are some ways you can be caring toward others in everyday situations?

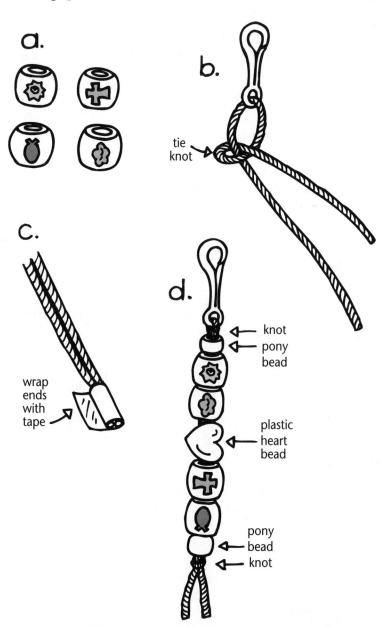

a.

b. tie knot

c. wrap ends with tape

d. knot / pony bead / plastic heart bead / pony bead / knot

"In the beginning God created the heavens and the earth. God created man in his own image... male and female he created them."
Genesis 1:1,27

"All have sinned and fall short of the glory of God."
Romans 3:23

"Jesus answered, 'I am the way and the truth and the life. No one comes to the Father except through me.'" John 14:6

"For Christ died for sins once for all...to bring you to God."
1 Peter 3:18

"Live a life of love, just as Christ loved us and gave himself up for us."
Ephesians 5:2

"In the beginning God created the heavens and the earth. God created man in his own image... male and female he created them." Genesis 1:1,27

"Jesus answered, 'I am the way and the truth and the life. No one comes to the Father except through me. If you really knew me, you would know my father as well.'"

John 14:6,7

The Way

The Truth

The Life

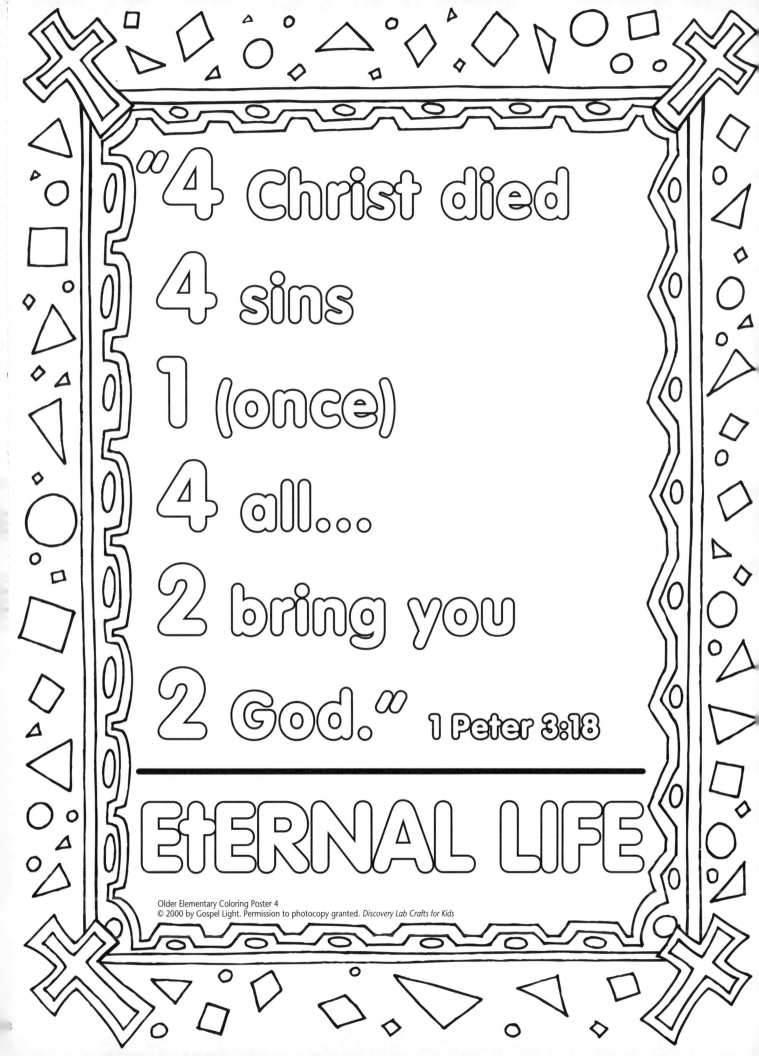

"4 Christ died
4 sins
1 (once)
4 all...
2 bring you
2 God." 1 Peter 3:18

ETERNAL LIFE

"Live a life of love, just as Christ loved us and gave himself up for us."

Ephesians 5:2

The MegaBuddy Award

_____

was a good friend at

_____.

Time-Traveler Award

_____,

we hope you had a great time visiting

_____.

Please come back again!

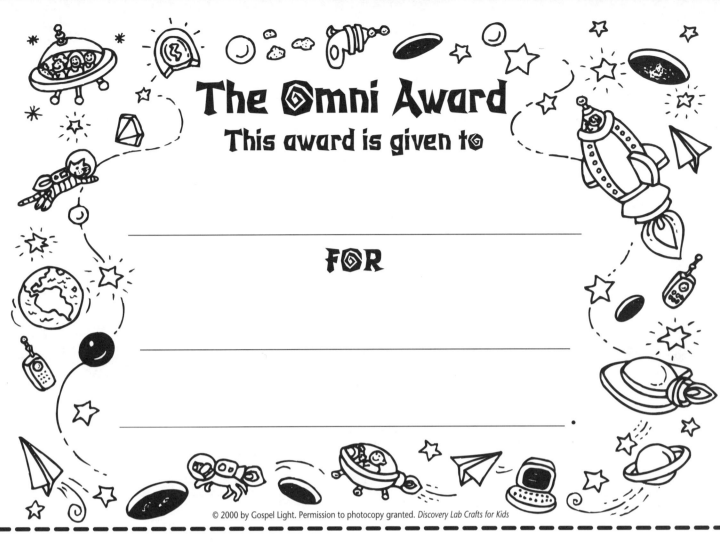

The Omni Award
This award is given to

_____

FOR

_____

_____

_____

SUPER GENIUS AWARD

_____

memorized all the Bible Memory Verses at

_____

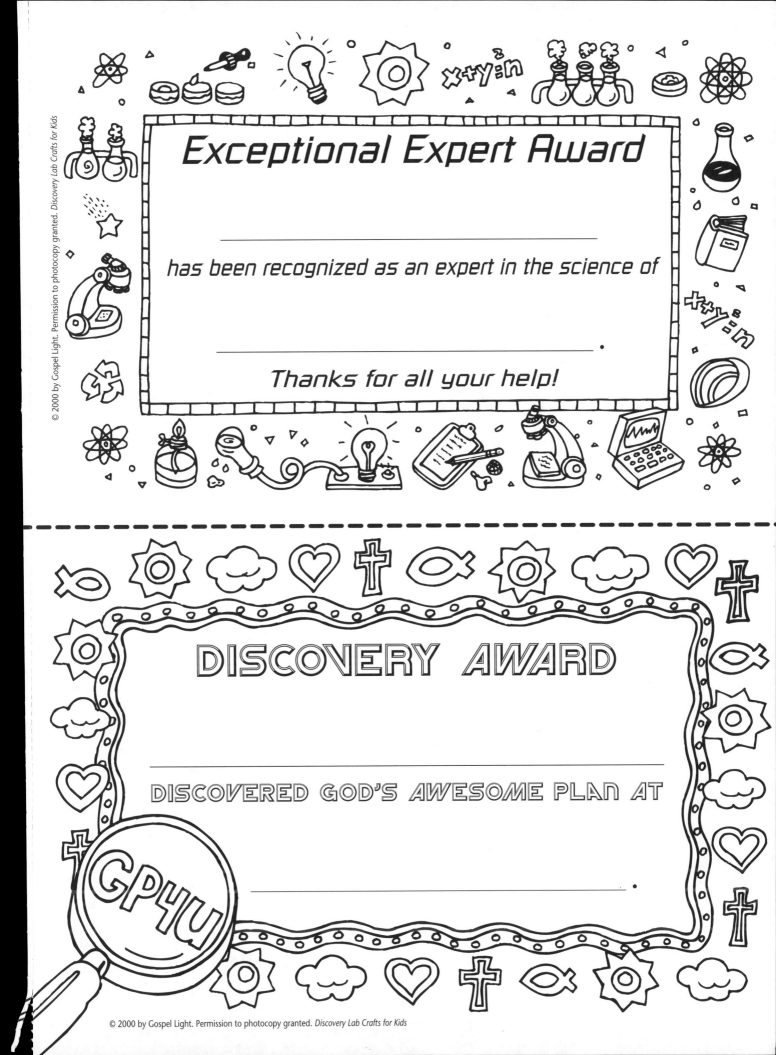

Exceptional Expert Award

_____

has been recognized as an expert in the science of

_____ .

Thanks for all your help!

DISCOVERY AWARD

_____

DISCOVERED GOD'S AWESOME PLAN AT

_____ .

GP4U

ATTENDANCE AWARD

PRESENTED TO

FOR ATTENDANCE AT

Place sticker here.

Place sticker here.

Place sticker here.

Place sticker here.

Place sticker here.

ECT

Sticker Poster

Transport To Truth

Index

Minerals & Rocks

by Barbara Brooks Simons

Table of Contents

What natural processes and forces form different types of rocks from minerals?

Rock of Ages

Diamonds are the hardest and purest mineral known on Earth. We use diamonds in many ways. Diamonds can be used as industrial tools to cut, drill, and polish other substances. But most people love them because of the way they sparkle and reflect light. Diamonds have always appealed to people's imagination. As gemstones, they are associated with royalty, romance, and riches.

The enormous blue stone known as the Hope Diamond is one of the most famous. A French jeweler bought the stone in India in the 1600s. At first it weighed over 112 carats. (A **carat** is a diamond's weight. One carat equals 200 milligrams, about 0.79 ounces.) Legend said that it came from the eye of an idol and that the stone carried a curse. A French king bought and recut the stone soon after. Since then the stone has rested on the hands, necks, and crowns of the rich, famous, and unlucky. In 1958, the Hope Diamond, thought to be one of the greatest treasures of all time, was given to the Smithsonian Institution, where it can be seen today.

How does such an enchanting gemstone form? Where does it come from? What is it made of? Could it really bring bad luck? The fascinating answers are in this book.

▼ Today the Hope Diamond weighs 45.52 carats. It is 25.6 millimeters long and 21.76 millimeters wide— about 1 inch by 7/8 inch.

▲ People admire diamonds for their beauty and their strength. In addition to jewelry, diamonds are used in industrial machinery and even dental drills.

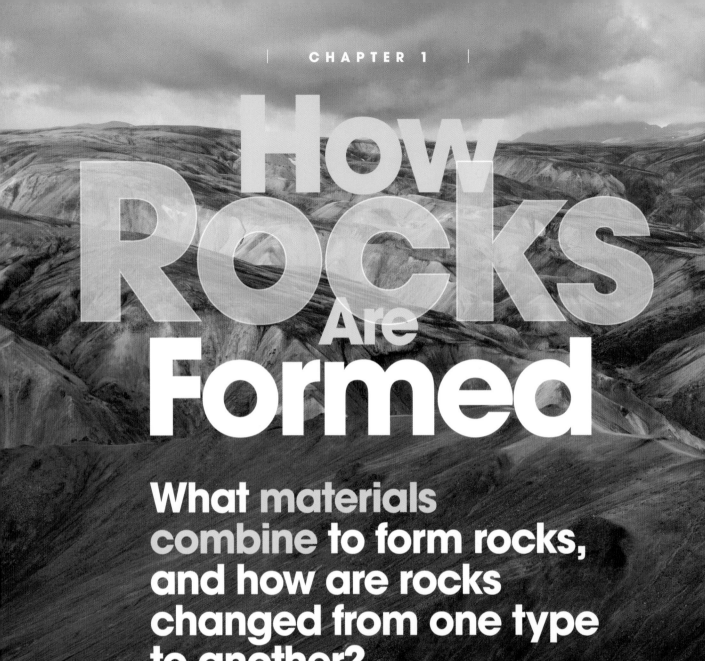

How ROCKS Are Formed

What materials combine to form rocks, and how are rocks changed from one type to another?

Galenite quartz

Gold

Mica

What Is a Mineral?

How are a sparkling diamond and a handful of table salt alike? Both are **minerals**. Minerals look very different from one another, but each has five important characteristics.

- A mineral is a naturally occurring solid.

- A mineral is **inorganic**. It does not come from a plant or animal.

- Almost all minerals have a **crystal** form. In a crystal, the atoms are lined up in an orderly, repeating pattern.

- Each mineral has a definite chemical composition. It may be made of one element or several, but its chemical formula is always the same.

- Each mineral has physical properties, such as color, luster, hardness, streak, cleavage, and heaviness, that help identify it.

Minerals That Form Rocks

Minerals are the building blocks of rocks. There are 3,000–3,500 different minerals on Earth. Only one hundred or so combine to form rocks. The most abundant mineral in Earth's crust is silica, also known as silicon dioxide. Other minerals can combine with silica to form a class of compounds called **silicates**. Ninety percent of the rocks in Earth's crust are made of just five groups of silicates.

▼ These are all examples of rock-forming minerals.

Calcite

Pyrite

Salt

Properties of Minerals

Here is a list of some of the physical properties to identify minerals.

- **Color.** Some minerals have a distinctive color. Malachite is brilliant green. Sulfur is smoky yellow.

- **Luster.** A mineral's luster is the way that it reflects light. For example, a metal surface can be shiny. Some nonmetals are dull, pearly, or glassy.

- **Hardness.** A measurement system called the Mohs scale sets up ten minerals as examples of relative hardness.

- **Streak.** Rubbing the edge of a mineral on an unglazed white tile (called a streak plate) will typically leave a streak of color. The streak may not be the same color as the mineral itself.

- **Cleavage.** Cleavage (KLEE-vij) is the tendency of certain minerals to break in a specific way. Mica, for instance, always breaks into thin sheets. The way the mineral cleaves, or splits, helps us identify it.

- **Heaviness.** Minerals have a specific gravity, or heaviness. Some minerals feel heavy in your hand because of their great density.

Some minerals have unusual properties. Magnetite and hematite are magnetic. Halite (rock salt) tastes salty (though you should never taste a mineral without knowing what it is). Some clay minerals smell earthy. Calcite and similar minerals fizz if you drop weak acid (such as vinegar) on them.

Science and Math

Mohs Hardness Scale

This scale rates ten minerals according to their relative hardness. But the intervals between the minerals are not mathematically even. For instance, diamond (#10) is actually some 40 times harder than talc (#1). Even without mineral samples, you can find relative hardness with a scratch test, using everyday objects. A mineral will scratch any substance with a lower number than itself on this scale. Likewise, it will be scratched by any substance with a higher number.

Mohs Hardness	Reference Mineral	Objects for Scratch Test
1	Talc	Fingernail
2	Gypsum	
3	Calcite	Copper penny
4	Fluorite	Iron nail
5	Apatite	Knife blade
6	Orthoclase feldspar	Window glass
7	Quartz	Steel file
8	Topaz	
9	Corundum	
10	Diamond	

Hands-On Science
Heating the Land and Water

Why do crystals form in different sizes? One reason is how quickly they grow.

TIME REQUIRED

1 hour to set up, 10-minute observation on several following days. Crystals may take up to a week to form.

MATERIALS NEEDED

- 2 small clear glass beakers
- Small saucepan
- Stove or burner
- Measuring cup
- Water
- Spoon
- Rock salt
- 2 pencils
- Nylon string
- Paper clips
- Refrigerator
- Hand lens

SAFETY

Always have an adult help you with the stove and the first steps of this experiment. Be very careful with the hot water and be sure to use protective goggles and heat-resistant gloves.

PROCEDURE

1. Clean and dry two glass beakers thoroughly. Be sure not to leave any residue inside the glass.

2. Heat about 1 cup of water to boiling. Remove from the stove or burner. Use a spoon to stir in about 1 cup of salt, or as much as the water will dissolve. Then let the mixture cool for 10–15 minutes.

3. Meanwhile, take two pencils. Tie a 6–inch piece of string around the middle of each pencil. Weight each string with a paper clip, so it dangles down.

4. When the water has cooled, slowly pour half the mixture into each beaker. Then place a pencil across the top of each jar, so the string dangles into the water.

5. Being sure to keep the mixture still, place one beaker in the refrigerator, and leave one beaker on the counter.

6. Create a table to record your observations of each beaker as the week goes on.

7. Continue to observe the beakers each day until the water has evaporated. Then use the lens to observe the crystals that form on each string.

ANALYSIS

1. How do the crystals that form in each beaker compare?

2. Based on your observations, what can you conclude from this experiment?

3. How do temperature and evaporation affect the formation of crystals?

How does this experiment relate to the difference in crystal size between rocks that cool on the surface and those that form deep inside Earth? (See Chapter 2.)

Uses of Minerals

Some minerals, such as topaz and garnet, are beautiful. The rough stones are cut and polished into gemstones. Other minerals are useful in industry and science. Some minerals are both useful and beautiful. For instance, quartz is the most common mineral in Earth's crust. Colored quartz, such as amethyst, are gemstones. Quartz is also used in watches and electronics.

Ores (ORZ) are minerals (and rock-containing minerals) that are mined to produce valuable metals or other materials. Iron ore, for example, comes from the minerals hematite and magnetite. Lead comes from an ore named galena. Aluminum comes from the ore bauxite.

Many nonmetal minerals are also used in industry. Very hard minerals, such as diamonds and rubies (a form of corundum), are used in tools for drilling and grinding. Sandpaper and emery boards both use corundum. Borax yields boron, which is used in laundry detergents and ceramics.

Clay minerals are used in many ways. Gardeners use the mineral vermiculite to help soil hold water. Kaolinite, a white, powdery mineral, is used in making fine china.

Some Important Minerals and Their Uses

Mineral	How It Is Used
Calcite	Forms marble and limestone; used in optical instruments
Chalcopyrite	Source of copper ore
Corundum	Rubies, sapphires; used for grinding
Fluorite	Source of fluoride; used in toothpaste and drinking water
Galena	Source of lead

Mineral	How It Is Used
Gold	Used in jewelry, dentistry, electronics
Hematite/ Magnetite	Sources of iron ore
Mica	Used in vacuum tubes, paints, and plastics
Quartz	Used in jewelry, watches, electronics
Sphalerite	Source of zinc

CALCITE CHALCOPYRITE CORUNDUM FLUORITE GALENA

GOLD HEMATITE MICA QUARTZ SPHALERITE

◀ Weathering and erosion transform rocks over time. These forces helped to shape Delicate Arch in Utah.

✔

checkpoint

Make Connections

What land formations near you have been shaped by weathering and erosion?

What Is a Rock?

As you have read, minerals are the building blocks of rocks. A rock is a hard, naturally formed, solid material that is a mixture of one or more minerals. Sometimes a rock also contains other substances like the remains of living things.

Most rocks are a mix of many minerals. Some contain just two or three. Slate, for instance, contains quartz, mica, and sometimes pyrite. Pure marble contains only calcite or dolomite.

We often think of rocks as solid and unchanging. Rocks are solid, but in fact, many rocks began as other types of rock.

Forces on Earth's surface and deep within it constantly change rocks and their characteristics. Weather conditions on Earth's surface can also change rocks slowly over time.

• Wind, water, and ice wear away rocks on the surface. This process is called **weathering**.

• Wind and water also carry grains of rocks and minerals away. This process is called **erosion**.

• In time, this sediment settles in other places. This process is called **deposition**.

11

Three Classes of Rock

Geologists classify rocks into three major groups, or classes, depending on how they were formed. Most rocks are formed when other rocks are changed by various processes. The minerals and other matter in the rocks are re-formed into new rocks in a series of changes called the **rock cycle**.

GRANITE (IGNEOUS)

- **Igneous rock.** These rocks are formed when hot, melted rock deep within Earth cools and hardens. Sometimes the molten rock reaches the surface and hardens there.

- **Sedimentary rock.** The processes of weathering and erosion break rocks down into smaller pieces, called sediment. The sediment might be sand at a beach. It might be mud at a lake bottom. It might be pebbles in a river. If these little pieces become cemented together, sedimentary rocks are formed.

SANDSTONE (SEDIMENTARY)

- **Metamorphic rock.** Deep within Earth, intense heat and pressure can change the minerals and materials in a rock. These forces act on both igneous and sedimentary rocks to change them into another form. A metamorphic rock can also be changed into a different form.

SLATE (METAMORPHIC)

The Rock Cycle

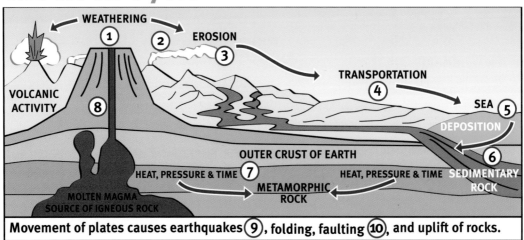

WEATHERING
① ② EROSION ③
TRANSPORTATION
④
VOLCANIC ACTIVITY ⑧
SEA ⑤
DEPOSITION
⑥
OUTER CRUST OF EARTH
HEAT, PRESSURE & TIME ⑦
HEAT, PRESSURE & TIME SEDIMENTARY ROCK
METAMORPHIC ROCK
MOLTEN MAGMA SOURCE OF IGNEOUS ROCK
Movement of plates causes earthquakes ⑨, folding, faulting ⑩, and uplift of rocks.

The Root of the Meaning
The word **igneous** comes from the Latin **ignis**, which means "fire." The words **ignite** and **ignition** are related, too.

Summing Up

- Minerals are naturally occurring, inorganic solids with a crystal structure and a definite chemical composition.

- Minerals are the building blocks of rocks.

- Physical characteristics such as color, streak, and hardness help identify a mineral.

- A rock is a hard, naturally occurring mixture of one or more minerals and other substances.

- Rocks are generally divided into three classes— igneous, sedimentary, metamorphic—depending on how they are formed.

- The rock cycle is a series of processes by which the materials in one type of rock are changed to produce a different type of rock.

Putting It All Together

Choose one of the activities below. Work independently, in pairs, or in a small group. Share your responses with the class. Listen to other students present their responses.

1 Discover what mineral resources are found in your community. Do local industries make use of them? Interview someone involved in that industry.

2 Minerals are used in many common household products, such as cleaners and paints. Read the labels on these products (at home or in a store) and make a poster displaying some of the products and a list of the minerals in them.

3 Reread page 10 and choose a favorite gemstone, such as ruby, sapphire, or turquoise. Research this stone to find where it is found and how it is processed and used.

If This Rock Could Talk . . .

CARTOONIST'S NOTEBOOK • ILLUSTRATED BY PETE PACHOUMIS

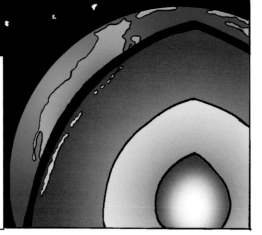

OUR STORY BEGINS TWO BILLION YEARS AGO AND 161 KILOMETERS BENEATH EARTH'S SURFACE, WHERE CARBON ATOMS BONDED TOGETHER WITH TRACE AMOUNTS OF BORON UNDER EXTREME HEAT AND PRESSURE TO FORM . . .

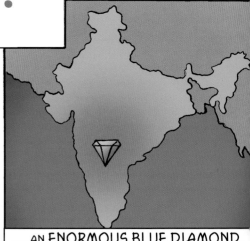

. . . AN ENORMOUS BLUE DIAMOND, WHICH WOULD ONE DAY SURFACE IN INDIA!

WOW! THIS IS HEAVY. DO YOU HAVE A BAG? . . . OR A BOX?

IN THE 1600s, A FRENCH MERCHANT NAMED JEAN BAPTISTE TAVERNIER BOUGHT A HUGE STONE. IT WEIGHED OVER 112 CARATS. LEGEND TOLD THAT THE STONE CARRIED . . . A TERRIBLE CURSE!

THIS STONE IS TRULY MEANT FOR YOU, YOUR GREATNESS!

IT IS VERY ME! BUT I WISH IT WERE SHAPED DIFFERENTLY . . .

THE MERCHANT SOLD THIS BEAUTIFUL STONE TO KING LOUIS XIV OF FRANCE. THE KING HAD THE DIAMOND RECUT AND NAMED IT "THE FRENCH BLUE."

MAGNIFIQUE!

C'EST, C'EST BON!

YOU SAID IT!

HE AND FUTURE KINGS WORE "THE FRENCH BLUE" FOR CEREMONIES.

During the French Revolution in *1791*, King Louis XVI and Marie Antoinette tried to flee France with the crown jewels... They did not make it... and "the French Blue" disappeared...

George IV, 1830

Anybody want to buy some fierce bling?

Henry Philip Hope, 1839

I'll take it... and rename it!

Lord Francis Hope, 1899

Blasted curse!

Joseph Frankels, 1901

Drat!

Sultan Selim Habib, 1909

Phooey!

...Until some years later King George IV of England acquired the cursed "French Blue." The king died in debt in *1830*. The jewel was bought by Henry Philip Hope in *1839*, and renamed the Hope Diamond. The diamond passed through several hands. Its owners all died or lost their fortunes and had to sell it.

I don't believe in curses! Make it a necklace and I'll take it!

In *1911*, the diamond was bought by the heiress Evalyn Walsh McLean who wore the diamond as a necklace until her death in *1947*.

Wow! If this rock could talk...

In *1958*, the Hope Diamond was donated to the Smithsonian Institution in Washington, D.C., where it remains to this day...

The Hope Diamond has captured peoples' interest, and wallets, for centuries.

What are the physical properties of this rock that make it so special?

What other treasures found in nature do you think are precious? Why?

Igneo Roc

How are igneous rocks formed?

Extrusive Rocks and How They Form

Deep within Earth, rocks in the mantle melt and become extremely hot liquid, or molten. This molten rock beneath Earth's surface is called **magma**. Cooling magma can form two types of igneous rock: extrusive and intrusive. Which type forms depends on whether the magma cools very slowly within Earth's interior (intrusive) or more quickly on Earth's surface (extrusive).

Mount St. Helens, May 18, 1980

Some magma makes its way to the surface of Earth. It may flow out through a crack or weak spot in the crust, on land, or on the ocean floor. At other times, magma bursts violently through the surface when a **volcano** erupts. Molten rock on the surface is called **lava**. When lava cools, it forms different kinds of **extrusive rock**.

Most extrusive rocks are fine-grained. They contain very small crystals or none at all. The lava cools so quickly that large crystals do not have time to form. One example is obsidian, or volcanic glass. It is usually black and shiny, with no crystals. It breaks with sharp edges and a curved surface. Native Americans used sharp pieces of obsidian for knives and arrowheads. Pumice (PUH-mis) also cools instantly but forms from lava that is filled with gas. Unlike obsidian, pumice is full of air holes and is very light in weight.

Ring of Fire

A large group of volcanoes lies around the Pacific Ocean. There are about 452 volcanoes, most of them active. This area of volcanoes is called the Ring of Fire.

checkpoint

Read More About It

Use the Internet to find out more about the Ring of Fire, a belt of intense volcanic activity all around the Pacific Ocean.

RING OF FIRE

PACIFIC OCEAN

The most common extrusive igneous rock on Earth is basalt (buh-SAULT). It is fine-grained and usually black or another dark color. Basalt forms on the ocean floor and also the dark patches we see on the moon. Not all basalt comes from volcanoes. Early in Earth's history, slow floods of basalt built up cliffs and plateaus in many parts of the world.

Layers of lava and other material from a volcanic eruption build up mountains. Lava that is runny or watery erupts slowly, flowing down the mountain like a red-hot river. It forms low, flat shield volcanoes like those in Hawaii. Thicker, sticky magma may be filled with gases that explode violently. These eruptions send rocks and ashes into the air. Lava and ash form a typical cone-shaped volcanic mountain, like Mount Fuji in Japan.

Science and Math

Pie Charts

Pie charts (or circle graphs) are used to show the data for several categories within a given topic. The size of each slice in the pie represents the percentage of each category in the whole. This pie chart shows the percentage of each type of rock found in Earth's crust. Which type of rock is the most common? How much more common is it than the least common type of rock? Why do you think some rocks are more common than others?

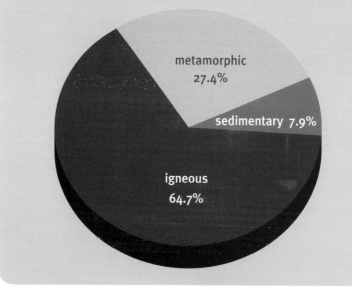

▲ Basalt is a fine-grained extrusive rock that forms on the ocean floor.

▲ Pumice is a lightweight rock formed by gas-filled lava. As it cools, the gases escape, leaving holes.

▲ Obsidian, which is black and shiny, is formed by quickly cooling lava.

Intrusive Rocks and How They Form

Some magma never reaches the surface. Instead, molten rock "intrudes" into spaces and cracks in the surrounding rock, and slowly cools and hardens there. It forms different kinds of **intrusive rock**.

Rocks that form very slowly deep underground are coarse-grained. Crystals have plenty of time to develop, so they are large and easy to see. Intrusive rocks that form closer to the surface may have finer grains.

Intrusive rocks take different shapes within the surrounding rock. Some are flat, table-like structures. These structures are called dikes and sills. Others are irregular in shape.

Granite is the best-known and most common intrusive igneous rock. Just as basalt makes up the ocean floor, granite is most important in the crust of the continents. Granite is also the main igneous rock in mountain ranges. The mineral crystals in granite—which are large enough to see—include quartz, feldspar, and mica. Its chemical composition varies. Other important intrusive rocks are gabbro and diorite.

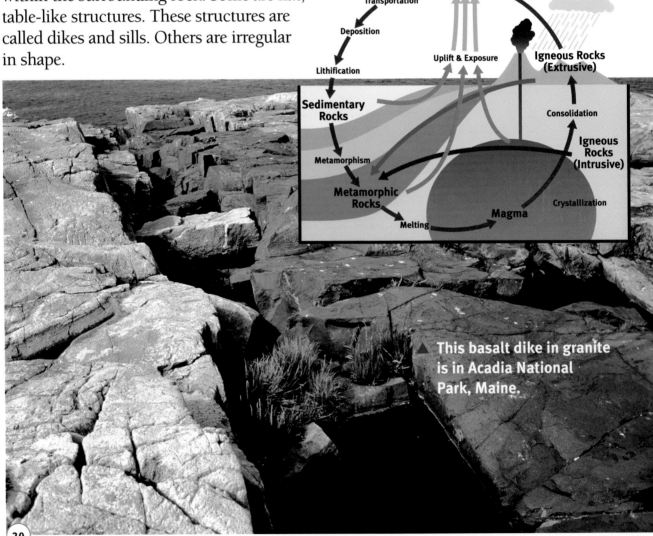

This basalt dike in granite is in Acadia National Park, Maine.

Because intrusive rocks form deep inside Earth over long periods of time, scientists cannot observe the actual process. However, intrusive and extrusive igneous rocks are made of the same minerals. Over time, erosion and Earth movements can bring these rocks to the surface. They become important features of Earth's landscape.

Sometimes, as a volcano stops erupting, magma clogs up inside the vent and hardens there. When the cone has eroded away, the hardened magma is left. It forms an isolated pillar called a volcanic neck.

▼ These granite rock formations are found in Yosemite National Park, California.

Science and Technology

Volcano Monitoring

When a volcano is known to be active, scientists watch its behavior carefully. Changes at the surface can show that magma is moving below it. A network of instruments measures these changes. A tiltmeter, for instance, shows changes in the slope of the volcano. Lasers supply other measurements of the surface. Seismographs record local earthquakes, which are usually the earliest warnings. Other instruments measure changes in electrical and magnetic fields. All these measurements help scientists predict a coming eruption and warn people nearby.

This volcanologist studies lava flow at Hawai'i Volcanoes National Park.

Igneous Rock
Landforms

▲ Mount St. Helens, Washing

Blahnukar, Iceland

The oldest rocks on Earth are igneous rocks. Granite (intrusive) is the underlying bedrock of the continents. Basalt (extrusive) makes up the ocean floors.

▲ Devil's Tower, Wyoming

▲ Ontario, Canada

▲ Columbia River Gorge, Oregon

Summing Up

- Igneous rocks form when magma hardens and cools. This occurs when magma reaches Earth's surface in a volcanic eruption or through a crack in Earth's crust.

- Lava cools quickly to form extrusive rock. Because the lava cools quickly, large crystals do not form.

- Most extrusive rocks are fine-grained, even glassy. They include basalt and obsidian. Basalt is the basic rock of the ocean floor.

- Sometimes magma cools and hardens very slowly below Earth's surface. It moves into other rocks and hardens there. That process forms intrusive rocks.

- The most common intrusive rock is granite, the bedrock of Earth's continents. Erosion and other processes can bring intrusive rocks to the surface.

▲ Mauna Kea, Hawaii

Putting It All Together

Choose from the following activities. Work independently, in pairs, or in a small group. Then share your responses with the class.

1 Make a diagram of the cross section of a volcano, including the magma chamber and the pipe or vents that allow magma to escape.

2 Use the Internet to research news stories about a volcanic eruption, such as Mount Redoubt in Alaska or Mount Pinatubo in the Philippines. Prepare a report for the class tracing the history of this eruption.

3 Make a simple chart of the major periods in the geologic time scale (Precambrian, Paleozoic, Mesozoic, Cenozoic), including their time spans and the dominant plant and animal life that lived in each period.

Sedime
RO

How are **sedimentary** rocks formed?

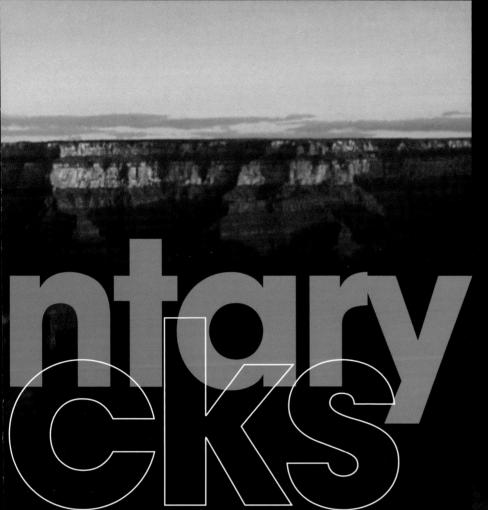

ntary
cks

How Sedimentary Rocks Form

Most of the rocks we see on the surface of Earth are sedimentary. In fact, sedimentary rocks make up about three-quarters of the rocks on Earth's surface. They are easy to recognize because they are made up of layers, often of different colors. You can easily see such layers in road cuts or in canyons. The layering is due to the way that sedimentary rock is formed.

Wind, water, and other forces break down rocks into smaller particles, called **sediment**. Sediment might include rock particles, sand, pebbles, and other small bits. Some material in sediment comes from living things. Bits of shells, bone, skeletons of sea animals, and plants can all go into the mix.

Particles are blown by wind or carried by water. Eventually they are deposited elsewhere. Most sedimentary rocks formed long ago in bodies of water. As layer after layer of sediment piles up, their weight presses and squeezes the layers tightly together. Minerals in the water fill in the spaces. Gradually they harden into a kind of glue or cement that binds the sediments together. The loose sediment has become rock.

A few sedimentary rocks do not form from particles of rock. Limestone, for example, is formed in water by minerals from shells and skeletons of sea animals. Coal forms from compressed plant remains, such as ancient trees. It does not contain mineral crystals.

Sedimentary rocks that form in water are originally deposited in flat, horizontal layers, like a stack of pancakes. This is known as the **law of horizontality.** When geologists study these rocks, they apply a related law called the **law of superposition**. In short, this law says lower layers are always older. Later, as Earth movements shift and fold the ground, the layers can be tilted or broken. Layers of rock may be turned over on top of each other, making it harder to tell their age.

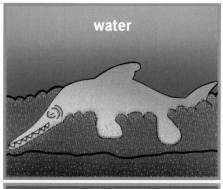

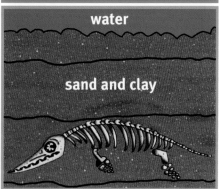

▲ **Sedimentary rocks that form in water are deposited in flat horizontal layers.**

Grand Canyon, United States

The Wave, in Vermilion Cliffs National Monument, is sedimentary rock that formed long ago when the southwestern United States (Arizona) was under water.

Beachy Head Cliffs, England

Ayers Rock, Australia

Common Sedimentary Rocks

Igneous rocks are at the base of Earth's continents and form the ocean floors. But the most common rocks exposed at the land surface are sedimentary. Depending on the sediment that forms them, sedimentary rocks can look very different. One difference is due to the size of the grains or particles in the sediment.

For instance, sand is made of tiny grains of quartz that feel gritty when you rub them between your fingers. You can see these fine grains in sandstone. By contrast, clay is so fine that it feels slippery, not gritty, on your fingers. When clay or mud turns to rock, it becomes shale. Shale is smooth and very fine-grained.

Other sedimentary rocks are made up of pebbles, gravel, and other larger rock fragments. Some fragments have sharp edges. Others have been smoothed and rounded by water. Conglomerate is a rock made up of a mix of large rounded pebbles. It is sometimes called puddingstone because it reminds people of a pudding full of raisins and plums.

The environment in which sediment was deposited and turned into rock causes other differences in sedimentary rocks. Sedimentary rocks can form in a desert from wind-blown sand that piles up into dunes. More often they form in water—on the ocean floor, a coral reef, or a riverbed.

The Root of the Meaning
The word sediment comes from the Latin *sedere*, which means "to settle."

checkpoint

Talk About It

Explain to a partner the process of how sedimentary rocks form.

Sediment often includes the shells and skeletons of sea animals, both ancient and modern. These contain the mineral calcite. When this material is buried and compressed, it forms various kinds of limestone. One is chalk, which is soft and very fine-grained. Over time, a coral reef, built by tiny sea creatures, also turns into limestone.

Another kind of limestone, called travertine, forms in caves. Water flowing underground dissolves limestone. Impurities add colors such as red and brown to the white limestone. Limestone-filled water flows through the cave and hardens on the cave walls and floors. This dripstone forms colorful pillars called stalactites and stalagmites.

TYPE OF PARTICLE	DIAMETER	SEDIMENTARY ROCK FORMED
GRAVEL/RUBBLE		
Boulder	Greater than 256 millimeters (10 inches)	Conglomerate
Cobble	64–256 millimeters (2.5–10 inches)	Conglomerate
Pebble	2–64 millimeters (.08–2.5 inches)	Conglomerate
Sand	.062–2 millimeters (.0025–.08 inches)	Sandstone
MUD		
Silt	.004–.062 millimeters (.00015–.0025 inches)	Shale
Clay	Smaller than silt	Shale

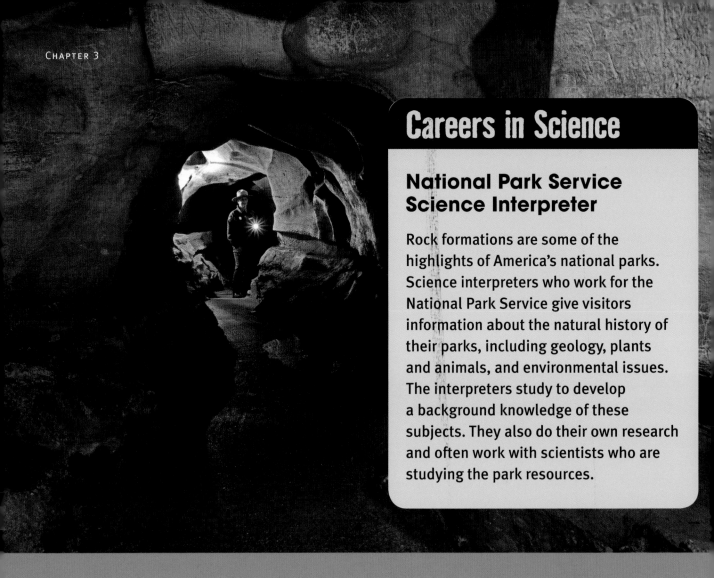

Careers in Science

National Park Service Science Interpreter

Rock formations are some of the highlights of America's national parks. Science interpreters who work for the National Park Service give visitors information about the natural history of their parks, including geology, plants and animals, and environmental issues. The interpreters study to develop a background knowledge of these subjects. They also do their own research and often work with scientists who are studying the park resources.

▲ Mammoth Cave in Kentucky is the largest cave complex in the world. Precipitated limestone decorates the caves with colorful stalactites and stalagmites.

Hands-On Science
How do different sediments act in water?

TIME REQUIRED

Day 1: 30 minutes plus 3 later observation periods
Day 2: Final observation of results

MATERIALS NEEDED

- Samples (about 1/3 cup each) of potting soil, gravel, and sand (or clay)
- Hand lens or magnifying glass
- Large clear glass jar with tight-fitting lid
- Water

SAFETY

When you have finished your experiment, dispose of the contents outside properly, especially the gravel. Do not pour the liquid down the sink, as it will clog the drain.

PROCEDURE

1. Study the samples with the hand lens or magnifying glass. Notice how they differ in color, texture, and particle size.

2. Put the samples in the jar one at a time. Add water till the jar is about three-fourths full.

3. Put the lid on tightly. Shake the jar until the samples are thoroughly mixed. Set the jar where it won't be moved.

4. After 30 minutes, look at the material in the jar. Check again an hour later, then two hours later.

5. Do not move the jar until the next day. Then observe it again. Which material sank to the bottom first? What did the material in the jar finally look like?

ANALYSIS

How and why are sedimentary rocks formed in layers? Explain using your results from the experiment.

Fossils and History

Fossils are traces, or remains, of once-living things. A fossil bone or shell is not always the actual object, however. Sometimes when a plant or animal dies, soil and sediments bury it, preserving its shape. Over time—perhaps millions of years—minerals from the soil slowly replace the harder parts of the organic, or living, material. That includes bones, teeth, or even pieces of wood. The minerals produce a rock-like copy.

Softer parts, such as a leaf or feather, rot away. But they still may leave an imprint, or mold, in sand or mud that eventually hardens into rock. An animal may leave behind a footprint, or even waste. These are called trace fossils.

Sedimentary rocks—especially limestone—are the best place to find fossils. Fossils are rare in other types of rock. Often heat or pressure destroys such traces.

Fossils are valuable clues to Earth's history. Scientists have several ways to find the age of a fossil. One way is to compare fossils found in similar rock layers. If the rock layers were undisturbed, fossils in the lower layers are older than those in upper ones. Another technique is to compare fossil species found in different places. That can help establish the dates of the rock layers and the time when the plant or animal lived.

Science to Science: Earth Science and Biology

What We Can Learn from "Ida"

Fossils tell scientists much about Earth's history. They are also keys to human history and evolution. "Ida" is a tiny fossil skeleton of a 47-million-year-old female primate, recently found in Germany. Her scientific name is Darwinius masillae.

Humans, monkeys, and apes belong to one group of primates. Lesser primates, like lemurs, belong to another group. Ida seems to be the earliest known example of the group that includes humans. She has nails, not claws. She has opposable thumbs.

The discovery is important in other ways, too. Ida's fossil skeleton is very complete, with hair and stomach contents still visible. (She ate fruit and leaves.)

Paleontologists in Orchard, Nevada, dug up the remains of a ten-million-year-old rhinoceros.

An **index fossil** is a plant or animal species that scientists have already identified. They know that it lived at a certain geologic time and died out fairly quickly. So they can conclude that other fossils found in the same rock layer as the index fossil are the same age.

Besides fossils, sedimetary rocks themselves can also be used to determine the age of the layer in which they are found. For example, if a rock of known age is also found in a layer of rock of unknown age, the mystery is solved.

These rocks can contain other clues to ancient Earth environments. Ripples may show that a rock formed near coastal waters or in a windy environment.

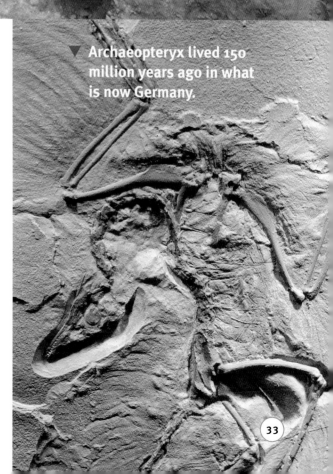

▼ Archaeopteryx lived 150 million years ago in what is now Germany.

33

Uses of Sedimentary Rocks

The most common sedimentary rocks are sandstone, limestone, and shale. For centuries, people all over the world have found ways to use them. Even though they are fairly soft, limestone and sandstone are widely used as building stones. For example, the brownstone houses built in many cities in the late 1800s were built of reddish-brown sandstone. Many "marble" floors in public buildings are actually polished limestone. (If you look at them carefully, you may see fossils.)

Limestone has many other uses in industry. Crushed limestone is used in road-building and in making cement. It can also be used in paper-making, chemicals, and glass-making. Even the coating on chewing gum may be limestone!

Sedimentary rocks and rock structures are the source of some of our most valuable energy resources. Some shales are rich in oil. Fossil fuels include coal, oil (petroleum), and natural gas. All form underground from the remains of ancient organisms. They are often found in oil shale and stored in sandstone or limestone.

▲ **This building in Petra, Jordan, was carved from limestone.**

Everyday Science

Acid Rain

Burning coal and other fossil fuels sends sulfur and nitrogen compounds into the air. They combine with water in the air, forming sulfuric acid and nitric acid. Rain, snow, and other kinds of precipitation carry those acids to the ground. Rain with a higher-than-normal acidity level is called acid rain. It can eat away the surfaces of buildings, statues, and even gravestones. It also harms trees. Soft sedimentary rocks, like limestone, are especially sensitive to acid rain.

Summing Up

- The most common rocks on Earth's surface are sedimentary rocks.

- Wind, water, and other forces wear away rocks into sediment, which includes particles of different sizes. Layers of sediment are then deposited, most often in water. As the layers pile up, their weight presses them tightly together.

- Minerals in the water form a kind of glue that hardens and binds the sediment into rock.

- Sedimentary rocks can be fine-grained or coarse-grained in appearance, depending on the particles that form them.

- Fossils of ancient plants and animals are most often found in sedimentary rocks. These give valuable clues to Earth's history.

- Sedimentary rocks are widely used in buildings, road construction, and other uses. Certain kinds yield energy resources.

Putting It All Together

Choose from the following activities. Work independently, in pairs, or in a small group. Then share your responses with the class.

1 Study the chart on page 29. Then make a collection of rocks of various sizes. Use the chart to classify them according to their particle size. Set up a classroom display with labeled examples of each size.

2 Tour your town or neighborhood to look for examples of sedimentary rocks (such as sandstone and limestone) used in buildings, floors, and even sidewalks. Take photographs (or make drawings) of six to eight different examples and group them into a poster.

3 Reread page 34 about the uses of sedimentary rocks. Research other uses and make a chart of those uses.

Metamorphic RO

What forces change other rocks into metamorphic rocks?

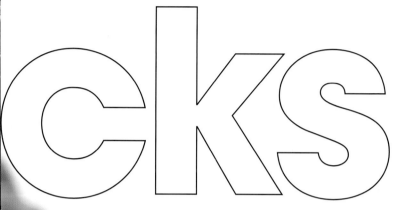

ESSENTIAL VOCABULARY
• metamorphism, page 37
• parent rock, page 37

How Metamorphic Rocks Are Formed

Metamorphic rocks get their name because they morph, or change, from one type of rock to another. The original rock, the **parent rock**, can be either an igneous or a sedimentary rock. It can even be a metamorphic rock that is then changed into another type of metamorphic rock. (Look back at the diagram of the rock cycle on page 12 to see the different paths along which these changes can take place.)

This process of **metamorphism** is caused by a combination of intense heat and pressure, usually deep within Earth. Very hot water and other liquids can also play a part. Metamorphism can change both the texture and the chemical composition of the original rock. Its crystals are changed. New minerals may be formed. The size of grains change. However, the parent rock does not melt completely.

The Root of the Meaning
The word **metamorphism** comes from the Greek *meta*, which means "to change" and **morph** which means "form."

▶ This flow chart illustrates one way in which rocks can go through different stages of metamorphism. Note that schist can also form from other types of rock, depending on their mineral content. Gneiss can also form from granite, an igneous rock.

- shale, a soft sedimentary rock
- slate, a dark metamorphic rock that splits in flat layers
- phyllite, a striped metamorphic rock with crystals of mica
- schist, a harder rock, with large mineral crystals
- gneiss (NISE), a coarse-grained rock with parallel bands of minerals

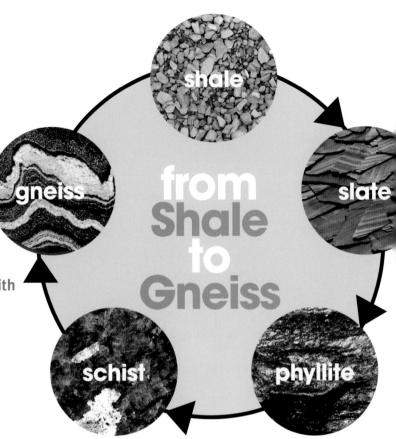

from Shale to Gneiss

Everyday Science

Is the lead in your pencil really the metal lead? No, it's a soft, shiny metamorphic rock called graphite. Graphite is pure carbon, usually metamorphosed from sedimentary rock. With enough heat, pressure, and time, this humble rock may eventually become a diamond.

Once a metamorphic rock has formed, it may be heated or squeezed still more. The process of metamorphism continues. It changes one metamorphic rock into another. This can continue through several stages. The process takes place gradually. Sometimes it is hard to classify a rock because the differences between one stage and another are not clear-cut.

Metamorphism can take place about eight kilometers (five miles) or more beneath Earth's surface. Therefore, scientists cannot observe it. Since metamorphism may take millions of years, scientists cannot time how long it takes for changes to occur. However, certain kinds of changes in the minerals can indicate the conditions in which the new rock formed.

Types of Metamorphic Rock

Metamorphism changes and rearranges the crystals and structure of rocks in two general ways. The resulting rocks are described as either foliated or nonfoliated.

Foliated rocks have a striped or layered appearance. Heat and pressure combine to force the crystals into parallel bands. The crystals are parallel to each other, and all point in the same direction. Pressure has flattened the grains. As its name suggests, banded gneiss is typical of a foliated rock. Slate and schist are also foliated.

By contrast, the crystals in nonfoliated rocks are arranged more randomly, without a definite pattern. The surfaces of these rocks look grainy, like grains of sugar, or marbled.

Marble is metamorphosed from limestone. If it forms from pure limestone, marble is white. Impurities can give marble a speckled surface of pink, black, or other colors.

Quartzite comes from sandstone but is much harder than its parent rock. While it looks something like marble, it is harder. Heat forces the grains of quartz in the sandstone tightly together.

Everyday Science

Metamorphic Coal

Starting from thick layers of wet plant materials, coal goes through four later stages. Peat, made up of compressed plants and leaves, becomes soft brown coal, or lignite. It then turns into ordinary bituminous coal, which is a sedimentary rock. Finally, coal metamorphoses into the hard, shiny coal called anthracite.

foliated

nonfoliated

Uses of Metamorphic Rock

Marble has been used for buildings and sculptures for centuries.

▲ Parthenon, Athens

Washington Monument, Washington, D.C.

▼ Trevi Fountain, Rome

Arc de Triomphe, Paris

checkpoint

Visualize It
Think about the physical differences between each type of rock. Then create a table. Draw examples of each type.

40

Summing Up

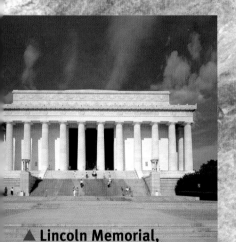

▲ Lincoln Memorial,
Washington, D.C.

• Metamorphism is the process by which heat and pressure change an original rock (parent rock) into a different type.

• It can work on an igneous, sedimentary, or even another metamorphic rock.

• Metamorphism changes the texture, structure, and the chemical makeup of the rock. It can create new minerals.

• Since the process takes place over time and deep within Earth, scientists have never been able to observe it.

Putting It All Together

Choose from the following activities. Work independently, in pairs, or in a small group. Then share your responses with the class.

1 Visit local parks and art museums to find examples of metamorphic rock—especially marble—used in statues and fountains. (Museum labels tell you what stone was used.) Create your own picture essay, like the one on page 40.

2 Research a famous sculptor of the past who created marble statues. Write a short report or biography describing how this sculptor got marble and what famous works he or she created. (Possible subjects are Michelangelo, Bernini, or Edmonia Lewis.)

3 Make a poster comparing the three main classes of rocks: igneous, sedimentary, and metamorphic. Include how each is formed, where it is found, distinctive appearance, major types, and uses.

Conclusion

The Hope Diamond was said to bring bad luck. It is true that many who owned the blue jewel died or lost their fortunes. Whether that was coincidence or a curse is hard to say. Cursed or not, few minerals and rocks have stories as celebrated as the Hope Diamond. But each type of rock has a beauty and fascinating history all its own. Igneous rocks like basalt and granite form from molten lava deep in Earth. Sedimentary rocks like coal, limestone, and shale are formed by layers of minerals, animal remains, and vegetation. Metamorphic rocks like marble, slate, and diamond begin as other types of rock. Then they are transformed by heat, pressure, and time.

Together, these minerals and rocks make up the landscape in which we live, the ground on which we stand. They supply resources. We use rocks and minerals in many different ways. Rocks and minerals are an important part of Earth's history.

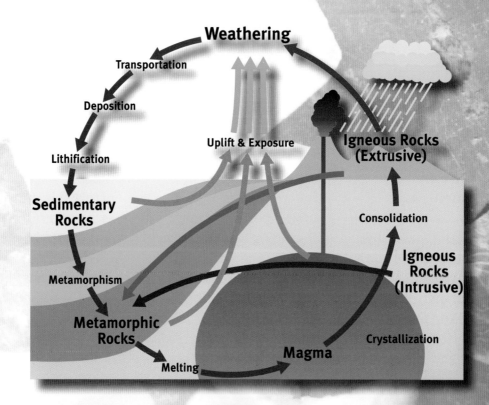

" **The curse is a fascinating part of the story of the Hope Diamond that has helped to make the diamond as famous as it is. But as a scientist, as a curator, I don't believe in curses.**"

—Jeffrey Post,

geologist and curator at the

Smithsonian Institution

How to Write a Biography

A biography is the story of a person's life, written by someone else. A full-length biography can take up an entire book, even several books. Other shorter biographies, such as those in a reference book, include just the highlights and important facts about that person's life.

Before choosing the person you want to write about, ask yourself these questions:

- Why is this person important or interesting or famous?

- When did this person live?

- What did this person accomplish?

- Why should we know about this person today?

Follow these steps:

- **Choose a subject.**
  Pick a person in science that you admire or want to know more about.

- **Do research about the person.**
  Gather your information from good sources—reliable Internet sites or well-researched books. Ask a librarian if you need help.

- **Make a plan or outline.**
  Your biography will be short, about three paragraphs. Organize your research. Decide what to include and what to leave out. Introduce some of your subject's accomplishments at the beginning, to catch a reader's interest.

- **Write a draft.**
  Include details to show how this person achieved his or her goals.

- **Edit, revise, and proofread.**
  Review your first draft. Does it make sense? Is it clear? Leave out unnecessary information. Proofread your final draft for spelling and grammar.

John Wesley Powell

John Wesley Powell (1834–1902) was a soldier and explorer, but most of all he was a scientist. Growing up on a farm, he became interested in natural history. He collected specimens of minerals, birds, and plants. He later became a teacher in a small Illinois town.

Powell's family strongly supported the abolitionist movement to end slavery. Just before the Civil War began, the young teacher studied military science and engineering. He enlisted in the Union army as soon as President Lincoln called for volunteers. Powell was wounded at the Battle of Shiloh, losing part of his right arm. He stayed in the army and became an outstanding officer. Even during war, Powell studied natural history, collecting fossils and local shells.

After the war, Powell became a professor of geology. The U.S. government was exploring new territories in the West. In 1869, Powell headed an expedition to explore the Colorado River and its canyons in small rowboats. From a second expedition two years later, he brought back maps and photographs. From 1881 to 1894 Powell was head of the U.S. Geological Survey. His work introduced Americans to the Grand Canyon and the geology and peoples of the American West.

Glossary

carat (KAIR-ut) *noun* a unit of weight for diamonds and other precious stones (page 4)

crystal (KRIS-tul) *noun* a solid in which the atoms are arranged in an orderly, repeating pattern (page 7)

deposition (deh-puh-ZIH-shun) *noun* the process by which wind and water carry pieces of rocks and minerals to other places (page 11)

erosion (ih-ROH-zhun) *noun* the washing or carrying away of rocks by wind or water, usually over a long period of time (page 11)

extrusive rock (ik-STROO-siv RAHK) *noun* a type of igneous rock that forms when lava cools on Earth's surface (page 18)

fossil (FAH-sul) *noun* the remains, or traces, of an ancient plant or animal preserved in rock (page 32)

index fossil (IN-deks FAH-sul) *noun* a fossil geologists use to date other specimens (page 33)

inorganic (in-or-GA-nik) *adjective* not produced by a living organism (page 7)

intrusive rock (in-TROO-siv RAHK) *noun* a type of igneous rock that forms when magma hardens beneath Earth's surface (page 20)

lava (LAH-vuh) *noun* molten rock that reaches Earth's surface (page 18)

law of horizontality (LAW UV hor-ih-zahn-TA-lih-tee) *noun* principle that says that sedimentary rock layers form in flat, horizontal layers (page 26)

law of superposition	(LAW UV soo-per-puh-ZIH-shun) *noun* principle that says sedimentary layers of rock are deposited in a time sequence with the oldest at the bottom and youngest at the top (page 26)
magma	(MAG-muh) *noun* molten rock in Earth's interior (page 17)
metamorphism	(meh-tuh-MOR-fih-zum) *noun* a process in which heat and pressure change one type of rock into another (a metamorphic rock) (page 37)
mineral	(MIH-nuh-rul) *noun* a natural inorganic solid with a crystal structure and definite chemical composition (page 7)
ore	(OR) *noun* rock that can be mined to produce metals or other useful minerals (page 10)
parent rock	(PAIR-ent RAHK) *noun* the original rock from which a metamorphic rock is formed (page 37)
rock cycle	(RAHK SY-kul) *noun* a model of the processes by which one type of rock is changed into another (page 12)
sediment	(SEH-dih-ment) *noun* small particles of rocks, soil, shell, and other material carried and deposited by wind and water (page 26)
silicate	(SIH-lih-kate) *noun* a compound of silicon, oxygen, and usually one or more metals (page 7)
volcano	(vahl-KAY-noh) *noun* an opening in Earth's crust where magma reaches the surface; also the hill or mountain formed by lava, ash, and rocks ejected through the opening (page 18)
weathering	(WEH-thuh-ring) *noun* the process by which wind and water wear away rocks on Earth's surface (page 11)

Index